BEYOND THE
PASSION

TO: MS ANNETTE WUTOH

19/3/16

BEYOND THE PASSION:

WHAT IT TAKES TO ACHIEVE SUCCESS IN BUSINESS

Why 'following your passion' is not all you need to do to truly become successful.

Victor Kwegyir – MSc
International Business Consultant,
Coach, Mentor & Speaker

Beyond The Passion
© 2016 by Victor Kwegyir

Published by VicCor Wealth Publishing
www.vikebusinessservices.com

First Edition
ISBN: 0956770673
ISBN-13: 978-0-9567706-7-7
ISBN-13: 978-0-9567706-8-4 (E-book)

PATHWAY TO BUSINESS SUCCESS SERIES

Printed in the United Kingdom and the
United States of America

To request Victor for speaking engagements, interviews, mentoring, proposal writing, one-on-one coaching, ghostwriting or consultation services, please send an email to: victor@vikebusinessservices.com.

Victor's books are available at special discounts when purchased in bulk for promotions or as donations for educational and training purposes.

ADDITIONAL PUBLICATIONS BY VICTOR KWEGYIR

**Pitch Your Business Like A Pro:
Mastering The Art Of Winning Investor
Support For Business Success**
(Pathway to Business Success Series)
by Victor Kwegyir

**The Business You Can Start:
Spotting The Greatest Opportunities In The
Economic Downturn**
(Pathway to Business Success Series)
by Victor Kwegyir

**You've Been Fired! Now What?
Seize The Opportunity, Creatively Turn It Into
A Successful Reality**
by Tonia Askins and Victor Kwegyir

DEDICATION

I dedicate this book to all my valuable clients, attendees to my seminars and those in my network across various platforms, who are working hard at their dreams to create successful and vibrant businesses across the nation and around the globe. To all of you entrepreneurs and business owners at all levels of growth, continue to be as exceptional as you are. You are very much appreciated and have earned my continued respect and support.

ACKNOWLEDGMENTS

I am grateful to everyone who has been there for this journey and to everyone who has inspired me with their encouragement and helped me to write this book, another exciting resource for entrepreneurs, business owners and aspiring entrepreneurs.

I am always grateful to God for every ounce of strength, wisdom and ability to do my work; to my pastor, Pastor Matthew Ashimolowo, President and Senior Pastor of Kingsway International Christian Centre (KICC), for continued inspiration to strive for excellence and explore possibilities to make an impact in our generation; to my great friend Michael Ajose, for his friendship, prayers, encouragement, and continued support; to Mrs. Kemba Agard, my department head at KICC, and a great help and encourager; to my wife and family for everything they do to support a husband, son, uncle and brother; Cyrus Webb, President of Conversations Media Group; Katherine Waddell, host of 'This Needs To Be Said', TV Show, and to Pastor Dr Dipo Oluyomi - KICC, Pastor Ade D'Almeida - KICC, Pastor Esther Dunmoye – KICC, Pastor Emmanuel Appenteng, Freda Lutterodt, Tonia Askins, and Mr and Mrs Joseph Babatunde, for their prayers, encouragement and support. You have all contributed in many ways to make the journey exciting and fulfilling, both professionally and spiritually. THANK YOU all once again!!!

TABLE OF CONTENTS

WHAT PEOPLE ARE SAYING

"It takes more than passion to sustain your business. When you took the leap and took the risk on yourself to live your passion you thought that would be enough. The truth is that this is only part of it. The other part is a knowledge investment. Take what you learn and apply it, daily. This is what helps you keep the passion."

- Katherine Waddell,
host of 'This Needs To Be Said', TV Show

"I have always known that I had been given gifts that I wanted to share with the world, be it through my art, writing or my communication skills but having those abilities wasn't enough. I had to find a way to not just do what I loved but to make it work for me. My passion for life definitely spurred me forward but the research, preparation and the work behind the scenes is what got me to where I am today. To date, I have interviewed some of the biggest names in the world, garnered a fan base of millions for my radio show and each day have thousands that I interact with through social media. My journey is a perfect example of where passion, purpose and perseverance come together to create the brand I have been building for the past 12 years."

- Cyrus Webb, President of Conversations Media Group

"I believe in the saying 'I need to love what I do and make money doing it!' so that's exactly what I set out to do. Even though it's based on passion, it has taken development of various skill sets and a bit of gracefulness and trusting my God-given instincts. Development of the skill sets are key whether it's negotiating or public speaking and of course I will always have room for improvement. Life has a lot to teach us and I have a lot to learn. Passion is the blood in my veins but the mind is required to think and learn, my hands are required to work, and my heart is required to keep me strong. Yes, indeed it takes more than passion."

-Tonia Askins, The Expert Cultivator, Tonia Askins
International

"I have always had an entrepreneurial spirit and I thrive on ideas and bringing them to life. Through my experience in business, I've learnt that creativity and ambition is not always enough to make your business successful. A good business advisor, marketing and someone to give you a reality check and support is important. Be organized and manage your time well because everything is your responsibility. Remember and accept that no one will have the passion and belief that you do. Be persistent and see mistakes as something to evolve from and bring you closer to your dream. And don't forget to rest and find time for you as this is important for focus and drive and to help you to come up with ideas and overcome any obstacles."

Nzinga Graham- Smith, Director of Queen of the Crop

INTRODUCTION

Over the years, I have read and listened to many business and motivational speakers and even challenged business people to 'follow their passion' when identifying and pursuing a business opportunity. Passion is touted as one of the quickest routes for launching or starting a new business. Others have suggested it is one of the predictors of whether a business will succeed or not.

I think the argument sounds appealing to many because it affords the aspiring entrepreneur an easier option of where to start as almost everyone has a passion of some sort or the other.

I have also come to appreciate that when you take passion out of the equation it becomes more challenging for many people to identify a realistic and easy starting point, especially when they have not yet identified for themselves what it is they can do, let alone turn into a successful business.

Like many people, although I believe in the significant role passion plays in helping one start and grow a successful business, it is simply only one of a list of things that help a would-be business owner or an aspiring entrepreneur to get started.

For instance, whereas a person seeking a career change in a developed country weighs up the prospects of owning a business and is driven by the desire to achieve financial freedom or to become their own boss etc., most aspiring entrepreneurs in less developed economies launch a business out of necessity, ready to take on anything as a means of survival.

This partly explains why it is no surprise that according to 2015 research by the UK-based business-networking group, Approved Index, the top 10 entrepreneurial countries are developing nations. Australia is the first developed country to appear on the list at number 26, with the UK and the USA at numbers 33 and 37, respectively.

The next question is, if passion has such a huge effect and helps to start a business, is it enough to make a business successful?

This book sheds light on why passion is only one ingredient in the quest to grow successful businesses. In all the years I have worked with entrepreneurs, start-ups and business owners, I have seen how passion got many started and how the lack of other skills, abilities, systems and structures contributed to the struggle to keep going, and in a lot of cases caused the business to fold. Lack of passion is also among the main reasons why many start-ups have never grown beyond the start-up stage, two, three, and even five years on.

This book is intended to help you to grow your start-up from a new business to a profitable successful business. I see no reason why you can't do this because, as it turns out, the passion which drives established entrepreneurs is the same passion we ourselves possess. It is common sense that if we haven't yet succeeded as they have, we need to consider what factors other than passion support their pursuit for success in business.

It's time to engage a higher gear and add to your passion to drive your business to greater success.

Let's do it!

CHAPTER 1

PASSION GIVES YOU THE IDEA, NOT A BUSINESS!

"Having a great idea is fantastic, but there's a very big difference between an idea and a business." **Deborah Meaden** - Dragons' Den millionaire investor

The word passion invokes a lot of emotion depending, of course, on the context in which it is used or the conversation going on at the time of its mention. Among the many definitions that are relevant to the topic of business are these from the English Oxford Dictionary: *"an intense desire or enthusiasm for something"* and the Cambridge English Dictionary: *"an extreme interest in or wish for doing something, such as a hobby, activity, etc."*

It can therefore be deduced that passion for business can simply mean an intense desire or enthusiasm for business or an extreme interest in, or wish for doing, business.

> PASSION FOR BUSINESS CAN SIMPLY MEAN AN INTENSE DESIRE OR ENTHUSIASM FOR BUSINESS OR AN EXTREME INTEREST IN, OR WISH FOR DOING, BUSINESS.

The question is, does every person who goes into business do it because of their passion for it? I don't think so. From the many interviews I've conducted among clients or the lessons from other entrepreneurs and stories I have read, it is clear to me that not everyone goes into business on the wings of a passion for business or to pursue a specific line of business.

I can tell you from firsthand experience that passion was not what drove me to start my business. Neither was it passion that originally led me to what I now do for a living. As I have said on countless occasions on many of the international radio shows I've been privileged to be invited to participate in, I was literally 'pushed into' what I do now because it was the only line of business all my years of education and work experience offered me. Thankfully I had the qualifications, skills and experience and could manage with almost no physical or financial resources to start with.

My passion grew along the way and other aspects of my business such as coaching and authoring of books, which was never part of what I thought I was starting at the time, became an exciting part of what I do. In a nutshell, my business was driven by the need to generate income to survive doing whatever was the most familiar to me. Even so, with my background and experience, I had to put together a plan, set up a number of vital systems and structures, have a strategy to make it all work and have the right mind-set and leadership skills to run a successful operation.

I know of many others who embarked on the entrepreneurship journey because of factors such as:

1. The need to earn extra income to support main employment income.
2. The need to bring in income to survive after being laid off or finding oneself unemployed.
3. The desire to become their own boss.
4. The desire to become financially independent.
5. The need for flexibility in working hours, especially for a lot of mom-preneurs.
6. The desire to have or create a work life balance.
7. The way to achieving higher personal goals or ambition.

It makes sense to appreciate that although many entrepreneurs may have been drawn in by their passion to start a business, the question of what specific business opportunity to pursue or focus on is one that a lot of people find challenging to start with.

This is where the overrated advice of 'follow your passion' often comes in. Many speakers, coaches, consultants and thought leaders, such as myself, have unconsciously given the impression through their teachings that passion is the only thing one requires to make a success of a business dream, or any other dream for that matter.

It is therefore not a surprise to find many people jumping on board and running with an idea after hearing this without due consideration of the whole picture. I believe this has been the root cause for the high rate of start-up failures and lack of growth for many new businesses and even existing small businesses.

However, let's acknowledge that passion is an important starting point in identifying business opportunities as well as running a successful business operation. A few other reasons why passion is so important are:

> PASSION IS AN IMPORTANT STARTING POINT IN IDENTIFYING BUSINESS OPPORTUNITIES AS WELL AS RUNNING A SUCCESSFUL BUSINESS OPERATION.

- Passion can help you identify an opportunity that you can comfortably tap into because you love providing that service or producing that product, even if you are not paid for it.
- Passion is a necessary driving force to get you through to the other side when a business faces challenges (which is common to every business) and falls on hard times.
- Passion invokes confidence in you to drive the business.

- Passion helps you to lead by inspiring your team, infecting them with your enthusiasm and earning you respect.
- Passion enables your customers to feel the vibe and buy into what you are offering.
- Passion drives you to take risks even when the odds are against you.
- Passion is a major factor in pitching to investors and winning them over to support you, your business and your vision.

I have come across others who are critical of the idea of following your passion. One such notable individual is **Ben Horowitz**, the cofounder of Andreessen-Horowitz, one of the most successful venture capital firms in Silicon Valley, USA. Not too long ago, he gave a commencement speech at his alma mater, Columbia University. The subject of his speech was - *"Don't follow your passion, and the world is not going to hell in a handbasket and the class of 2015 is not required to save it."* This was interesting, the message is directly opposed to what well known and well-meaning entrepreneurs in the business world have said over the years:

Sir Richard Branson, founder of the Virgin Group: **"There is no greater thing you can do with your life and your work than follow your passions – in a way that serves the world and you."**

Steve Jobs, late CEO and co-founder of Apple: **"It [what you choose to do] has got to be something that you're passionate about because otherwise you won't have the perseverance to see it through."**

Lakshmi Mittal, CEO of Arcelor Mittal (the world's largest steel-making company): **"This is a learning from the business life that first of all you need to have commitment, dedication and passion for what you are doing."**

In his speech, Ben Horowitz explained that:

- Passions are hard to prioritize and as such they (the students) should rather pursue what they are good at which will be much easier to figure out.
- Passions change over time and as such are not reliable as a guide to the future.
- You may not be good at your passion. Just because you love doing something does not mean you are good at it.
- And finally, passion is self-centered. Over time people learn that what they take out of the world is much less important than what they leave behind.

This is an interesting perspective that makes a lot of sense and is worth considering.

The challenge is that, often due to resource and time constraints, many entrepreneurs have to juggle all aspects of managing a business at least until they can afford to hire the requisite staff. The problem becomes exacerbated when an entrepreneur, lacking some of the fundamental skills, refuses to acknowledge his or her limitations or even to appreciate the value or importance of those essential skills.

I have, on many occasions, met passionate entrepreneurs who are running full steam with an idea with limited knowledge of such essential things as primary target market; competition; pricing, selling, promotion strategies; cash flow management; branding; supplier management; right business mind-set; negotiations; and an understanding of their potential customers and how to best serve their needs.

I hope I have managed to establish the fact that, yes, a business idea can spring from one's passion, however, to run a successful operation a significant number of other skills and factors must be in place to grow the business to become a successful one.

In the next chapter we will consider why following your passion can give you an idea but it needs to pass the economic viability test to make it worth pursuing.

ABUSINESS IDEA CAN SPRING FROM ONE'S PASSION, HOWEVER, TO RUN A SUCCESSFUL OPERATION A SIGNIFICANT NUMBER OF OTHER SKILLS AND FACTORS MUST BE IN PLACE.

CHAPTER 2

PASSION GIVES YOU THE IDEA, BUT IS IT THE RIGHT TIME TO STEP OUT TO START THE BUSINESS?

"There's an entrepreneur right now, scared to death, making excuses, saying, 'It's not the right time just yet.' There's no such thing as a good time." **Kevin Plank, CEO, Under Armour**

The question of when to step up and out into your own business is one which has robbed many budding business owners of an exciting journey of entrepreneurship. There are those who have never taken the step because there has never been a 'right' time. For others, the timing was always right, but somehow, they never took the leap until a potential opportunity was missed or it was simply too late to step out.

The interesting thing is that if you are using economic conditions as your parameter, both downturn periods and boom time periods are arguably an ideal time to step out because both can support the argument for starting a business. (Check out my book "**The Business You Can Start**" for the full import of the argument.)

> **B**OTH DOWNTURN PERIODS AND BOOM TIME PERIODS ARE ARGUABLY AN IDEAL TIME TO STEP OUT BECAUSE BOTH CAN SUPPORT THE ARGUMENT FOR STARTING A BUSINESS.

On the other hand, if you are considering your options based on your own circumstances, then the factors to consider are subject to your personal situation. Why do I say that? For instance, if you have lost your job and have no regular income, this is a huge incentive to step out and creatively navigate the start-up process. Being unemployed may have its own financial constraints, especially if you are without adequate savings, and you will have to rely on your creativity and bootstring your way until you start making money from the business. It is, however, one of the very few times you will have the luxury of time to extensively research your idea for a business. The pressure of having no other source of income can be harnessed and channelled into a positive drive to push you to ensure it works out because there is no turning back.

> THE PRESSURE OF HAVING NO OTHER SOURCE OF INCOME CAN BE HARNESSED AND CHANNELLED INTO A POSITIVE DRIVE TO PUSH YOU TO ENSURE IT WORKS OUT.

If you are in employment do not make the mistake many make by resigning as soon as the 'aha!' moment strikes you especially if you do not have sufficient savings or financial support to fall back on. It is smart to maintain your job whilst working on your business on a part time basis until there is sufficient cash coming in to enable you to take care of your financial needs.

> MAINTAIN YOUR JOB WHILST WORKING ON YOUR BUSINESS ON A PART TIME BASIS UNTIL THERE IS SUFFICIENT CASH COMING IN TO ENABLE YOU TO TAKE CARE OF YOUR FINANCIAL NEEDS.

There are so many things you can do while still on the job, long before starting the business, such as researching, testing the business idea, analyzing the competition, familiarizing yourself with the industry, searching out the best suppliers with the best terms, building a network of experts and support systems and writing a business plan/proposal. Of course, this will mean making significant sacrifices in time as you still have to do your 'day' job. However, you are guaranteed that your sacrifices will pay off in the end.

When all is said and done, the best time to start your business, in addition to the above, is to assess your readiness, know when you are ready based on your personal circumstances, vision and preparation, and not necessarily on the external economic conditions. You don't have to know it all, but you must know at least the basics as addressed in this book and the dictates of your personal circumstances must guide you to the right timing.

THE BEST TIME TO START YOUR BUSINESS IS TO ASSESS YOUR READINESS, KNOW WHEN YOU ARE READY BASED ON YOUR PERSONAL CIRCUMSTANCES, VISION AND PREPARATION.

CHAPTER 3

PASSION GIVES YOU THE IDEA, BUT IS IT ECONOMICALLY VIABLE?

"Only when you combine sound intellect with emotional discipline do you get rational behaviour." **Warren Buffett**

LOOK FOR A GAP IN THE MARKET AND START A BUSINESS THAT PROVIDES A NEW PRODUCT OR SERVICE TO FILL IT OR IMPROVE ON AN EXISTING PRODUCT OR SERVICE

I believe that anyone can start a business. The question is, can anyone grow a business and become successful? That, I am not so sure of because success has to do first and foremost with whether the business itself is an economically viable proposition.

A good new idea is often the basis for starting up a business. It follows that after establishing that entrepreneurship is the way to go, you look for a gap in the market and start a business that provides a new product or service to fill it or improve on an existing product or service.

Thankfully, what you are passionate about, as discussed in Chapter One, can be one of the best ways to help you identify an opportunity and the drive to run with it. (For more ways to help you identify business opportunities why not check out my book

"The Business You Can Start" where I talk about *30 Ways Of Identifying Business Opportunities,* including 'following your passion'.)

> **W**HAT YOU ARE PASSIONATE ABOUT CAN BE ONE OF THE BEST WAYS TO HELP YOU IDENTIFY AN OPPORTUNITY AND THE DRIVE TO RUN WITH IT.

An idea is only good if it passes the 'economic viability test'. An idea or an opportunity which you cannot take advantage of economically is not the way to establish a successful business. Often you find that we become so consumed by the passion and excite-

> **A**N IDEA IS ONLY GOOD IF IT PASSES THE 'ECONOMIC VIABILITY TEST'.

ment to run with the idea that our judgment becomes clouded and hinders us from making informed decisions on whether the idea is worth pursuing economically or not.

So it is not enough to fall in love with an idea and pursue it. Rather, it is necessary from the onset to assess the viability of the business and its future potential because a viable business must be able to grow and become profitable over time and must also be able to transform itself, adapting to changing times and customer needs over its lifetime.

Asking yourself a few simple questions can make all the difference between succeeding and failing. For a business to be viable, you must be able to answer the following basic questions positively.

- Does my idea meet a specific need?
- Is it an answer to a specific question or does it solve a problem in people's lives?
- Am I able to produce or provide something good enough that people would be willing to pay for?

- Can I offer something different to what already exists?
- Can I produce the item or provide the service at a reasonable cost?
- Can I put a price on my products or services?

> IT IS NOT ENOUGH TO FALL IN LOVE WITH AN IDEA AND PURSUE IT.

- Can I make a profit at the price people are willing to pay for my products or services?
- Is what I want to offer going out of fashion or being taken over by new technology?
- Is it a regulated business and, if so, can I meet the requirements in a cost-effective way?

Realistically answering the above questions, understanding the market and needs of customers, and tailoring your products and services to meet these needs at the right price is a great way forward.

However, to effectively answer the above questions, you must also research other conditions out there.

Evaluate potential competition, keeping notes on what you find. A thorough assessment and market research at this stage will help you to establish whether there is a market for your product or service. Some of the basic questions you will want your brief market research to help you answer are:

- Is this product or service going to satisfy a market need?
- Who are my potential customers and where can they be found?
- What competition is out there? Is it direct or indirect, local, national, or international?
- How distinctive is my product or service from what is being offered by the competition?

- Can the product stand the test of changing trends or take advantage of them?
- Does the law of the land allow for such a business to be established?
- At what prices are consumers prepared to buy my product, and can I make a profit at any stage?

You will need to clearly define the specific range of products or services you can sell and how you will sell them. The right answers to the above questions can make a huge difference to how you set yourself up to start and grow the business.

Finally, whatever idea your passion has led you to pursue, you should make every effort to test whether it is going to be economically viable to run with it. Without that you will set yourself up for the monumental task of running with something that has no life as a business potentially bringing on yourself stress, debts, frustration, disappointment and loss of confidence in your ability to achieve anything.

I hope this process helps you to take your passionate idea to the next level. In the next chapter, we will highlight the need to assess the gap in the market and its potential size.

CHAPTER 4

PASSION GIVES YOU THE IDEA, BUT IS THERE A GAP IN THE MARKET?

"The reality is that very few businesses invent a market for their products and services. Many, however go on to reinvent markets by filling gaps with standout offerings." **Richard Branson**

Another very important consideration for an aspiring entrepreneur or business owner is the potential gap in the market. Ultimately I believe that it is only when your passionate idea meets a gap in the market that there is a potential business idea worth considering.

Often times, the excitement to follow the passion and the idea of owning a business can be overwhelming and make one lose sight of what actually makes a business succeed.

> THE IDEA OF OWNING A BUSINESS CAN BE OVERWHELMING AND MAKE ONE LOSE SIGHT OF WHAT ACTUALLY MAKES A BUSINESS SUCCEED.

To clearly appreciate the gap in the market, you must realistically ask these relevant questions and get satisfactory answers before you can run successfully with the idea.

- Is there a market for my product(s) or service(s)?
- If there is, what is the size of this market?

- Is the market big enough to accommodate a new entrant?
- If it is not, can you target a different market segment, region, or city or consider exporting internationally?
- Do you have enough information or knowledge about these markets? If not can you easily access the required information to inform yourself as you go along?
- Are you able to access your chosen market economically? And do you have the resources and capacity to meet the demand should your products or services be received favorably?
- Can you produce these products or services better than the businesses that already exist? How different are your offerings from theirs?
- Can you clearly differentiate yourself and position your business as a better alternative to what already exists?

When all is said and done, the key to finding a gap is:

- to identify a real problem;
- to have a clear understanding of what the problem is;
- to identify who actually faces this problem or consider that as a 'pain point';
- to come up with the best solution possible: that only you can deliver an excellent service or product in answer to the problem;
- to realistically assess if people who find this a real 'pain point' are willing and ready to pay for a solution;
- to ensure that you are equipped, skilled and qualified to deliver a valuable and sustainable solution;
- to identify a sizeable market sufficient to enable you to invest and turn out profit at some point, even if not right away, and to grow a thriving business in the process.

Favorable answers to these questions will set you on a better path to success in business. If the answers to some or most of the questions do not yield positive results there is a very good reason to revisit and revaluate the idea and the market critically. In the process, you may end up with something different from your original idea and this could turn out to be a more viable prospect worth pursuing.

The next chapter discusses another crucial consideration necessary to turn out a successful business and that is, do you know enough about the business industry?

CHAPTER 5

PASSION GIVES YOU AN IDEA, BUT DO YOU KNOW ENOUGH ABOUT YOUR INDUSTRY?

"There exist limitless opportunities in every industry. Where there is an open mind, there will always be a frontier." **Charles Kettering**

It is all very well being passionate about an idea and willing to run with it, after all, you have been bombarded with words of inspiration challenging you to follow your passion, but have you thoroughly researched your industry and do you fully appreciate how the market forces interact with each other?

It is important to understand that every business falls under an industry or sector category in any given economy. Not only that, there are expected standards, legal requirements, limits, levels of duty of care to potential customers and clients, and even procedures for addressing disputes.

Also worth noting is that most businesses fall under the juris-diction of certain trade associations, bodies and industry regulators. These often act as support networks which offer guidance and assis-tance as well as introductions to the dos and don'ts of the industry.

For instance, it is exciting being a person who is passionate about cooking. You are the one called upon to cater on special occasions for friends and family who are delighted to benefit from your skill. However, if you decide to turn your cooking into a home-based business, the kitchen you have used time and time again to cook great meals for your friends and family will have to be inspected and must meet certain standards before being issued a health and safety certificate. In some jurisdictions premises used for commercial food preparation are subject to annual checks from the relevant licensing bodies before the license is renewed and in certain regions of the world you will also be expected to undertake food and hygiene courses and pass various checks before being issued a license to be able to cook for the public. There are also standards for bottling, packaging, storing the packaged meals, condiments, etc., including tests to ascertain the quality and components of the ingredients and quantities applied to ensure they meet all health standards.

You will also be expected to know your responsibilities and rights as a business catering for the public such as how to display and label your food packages, storage methods and facilities, terms for resolving disputes or availing your products for testing by regulators, and what constitutes an offence that could end in your license being withdrawn.

UNDERSTANDING OF THE INDUSTRY YOU OPERATE IN AND THE STANDARDS GOVERNING THE PRODUCTS OR SERVICE YOU PROVIDE IS ABSOLUTELY NECESSARY FOR THE SUCCESS OF YOUR BUSINESS.

Thorough understanding of the industry you operate in and the standards governing the products or service you provide is absolutely necessary for the success of your business. You wouldn't want to start trading and spend time and resources to build a customer base only to be shut down, to have your products banned or to be sued for negligence because you did not do your homework.

By all means follow your passion and let it inspire you, however, as you assess the viability of your business, seriously consider the depth of your industry knowledge and the regulations that govern the running of a business like yours. Only by doing this can you guarantee your success for a long time to come.

The next important consideration to discuss is: how much do you know of the existing competition and how to address it?

CHAPTER 6

PASSION GIVES YOU THE IDEA, BUT DO YOU KNOW OR UNDERSTAND THE COMPETITION?

"Entrepreneurs often say they have no competition, assuming that's an impressive claim. But if you claim that you don't have competition, you either believe the market is completely inefficient or no one else thinks your space is valuable. Both are folly."
Reid Hoffman - LinkedIn co-founder

Another very important factor you simply cannot ignore is the competition.

In business there is always competition for the available customer or client base. Ignoring it won't do you any favors. The fact is that even if there is no direct competition there will definitely be indirect competition. The threat of a substitute product, for

> THERE IS ALWAYS COMPETITION FOR THE AVAILABLE CUSTOMER OR CLIENT BASE.

instance, competes indirectly with your product, business or service, and is often overlooked by new business owners. And at the core of all competition is the competition for the customer's cash.

For instance, a potential customer has a choice of buying your brand of sports trainers or a pair from Nike - your direct competitor if you are a producer of trainers. Or they may decide that although they need trainers they would rather buy a ticket for a trip, get a new tyre for their vehicle or buy a new mobile phone.

> **A**T THE CORE OF ALL COMPETITION IS THE COMPETITION FOR THE CUSTOMER'S CASH.

At each point in time there is competition going on for the limited cash in the potential customer's pocket. The question is, what is it about your products or services that will convince the customer to choose to spend their cash on your business instead of somewhere else?

Another essential consideration is, whether the barriers to enter your industry are high. Consider factors such as high capital costs, high production costs, high marketing costs, unique technology and patents, consumer acceptance and brand recognition, training and skills, shipping costs, tariff barriers and quotas. If you are in an industry where it's easy to enter and leave, it is bound to be a highly competitive industry.

It is very important to know your industry, the nature of the competition and what they are offering, to be able to strategically position yourself to attract more of the existing target market to do business with you instead of them.

> **I**T IS VERY IMPORTANT TO KNOW YOUR INDUSTRY, THE NATURE OF THE COMPETITION AND WHAT THEY ARE OFFERING, TO BE ABLE TO STRATEGICALLY POSITION YOURSELF TO ATTRACT MORE OF THE EXISTING TARGET MARKET.

Having said that, you should not be so consumed with the competition that you have no clear direction of where you are going yourself. It is better to be driven by your mission rather than the competition. Never be pressured by the competition, focus on the bigger picture and how much value you can deliver to your target market. *"Chase your dreams, not the competition."* **Jamal Edwards** - MBE

I believe that you can always compete in one of the following or combination of ways based on your industry.

- Quality and differentiation of your product;
- Quality and differentiation of your service;
- Price of the products or service;
- The value of what you are offering to your customer base;
- Branding recognition.

COMPETITION IS ABSOLUTELY NECESSARY FOR BUSINESS SUCCESS.

Although many entrepreneurs would like to shy away from the reality of some form of competition, it is absolutely necessary for business success.

It is argued that competition drives performance and innovation. That is simply because, if you are the only provider in your industry or region, you are more likely to become complacent and may not see the need to improve as essential for your success. Even if you are in a crowded market, you can only stand out and become successful by providing something different. Healthy competition always encourages and inspires change for the better which will distinguish your business from what already exists. Without it there is no incentive for businesses to seek to become better or more efficient. Promoting competition is generally seen as one of the best ways to promote and sustain consumer satisfaction. It is therefore something that benefits society as a whole, in the long run.

COMPETITION DRIVES PERFORMANCE AND INNOVATION.

In a US Supreme Court case (National Soc'y of Prof. Engineers v. United States 435 U.S. 679 (1978)) the court ruled that competition is 'the best method of allocating resources in a free market' and 'that all elements of a bargain-quality, service, safety, and durability-and not just the immediate cost, are favorably affected by the free opportunity to select among alternative offers'.

> **E**VEN IF YOU ARE IN A CROWDED MARKET, YOU CAN ONLY STAND OUT AND BECOME SUCCESSFUL BY PROVIDING SOMETHING DIFFERENT.

Some of the benefits of competition to a business and business owners:

- It forces you to educate yourself about the business and industry, not to talk of yourself.
- It helps you to avoid becoming complacent and to maintain a sense of balance as you consistently seek to innovate and become better which will inspire your team to push themselves to become better in driving the business forward.
- It offers you and your team the incentive to work harder to become more efficient and productive thus helping you to drive costs down which eventually means lower prices for your goods and services - something your clients and customer will very much appreciate.
- It promotes initiatives and the freedom to try things outside the box which inspires confidence and general well-being of the team and the business.
- It helps you to deliver better quality goods and services.
- It offers more choice and variety to the end consumer.

- It forces you to compete for customers by improving on your customer service delivery.
- It forces you to focus on your core audience enabling you to provide target offerings to your customers.

Knowing the competition and understanding how the market forces interact is an essential element in growing a successful business. To 'follow your passion' without fully grasping this element and the benefits to your business is not smart. It is time to acknowledge it and take up the challenge.

The right mind-set as a business person is the next important issue to address. Read on, as we explore the kind of thinking that will deliver a successful business to you in your journey.

KNOWING THE COMPETITION AND UNDERSTANDING HOW THE MARKET FORCES INTERACT IS AN ESSENTIAL ELEMENT IN GROWING A SUCCESSFUL BUSINESS.

CHAPTER 7

PASSION GIVES YOU THE IDEA, BUT DO YOU HAVE THE MIND-SET OR MENTALITY OF SUCCESSFUL BUSINESS PEOPLE?

"Success starts in the mind." **Dani Johnson**

Mind-set is said to be 'a person's way of thinking and their opinions', according to the Cambridge English Dictionary. It also describes the way a person interprets events around them given how they think. The mind-set of an entrepreneur is as important as the strategies they will employ in operating a business. An educated or informed person has a different mind-set and has every potential to think and approach situations differently. The right mentality, mind-set or thinking makes a lot of difference in business. You can be passionate and driven by your ideas, however, if your approach to business is informed by wrong thinking or assumptions, it won't take long to find yourself derailed along the way.

> THE MIND-SET OF AN ENTREPRENEUR IS AS IMPORTANT AS THE STRATEGIES THEY WILL EMPLOY IN OPERATING A BUSINESS.

Business is about providing solutions to people's problems by exchanging goods and services for the end user of the product and/or service's cash. However, to make this happen, a set of strategies and series of events must come into play to ensure that the process turns out profit to sustain lasting growth and success over time. To run a business successfully, an entrepreneur or business owner must adapt their thinking to time tested ways of analyzing situations, processing available information and making the right judgments. Viewing things through the eye of successful business thinking is a huge determining factor in whether an entrepreneur will succeed or not in business.

> To run a business successfully, an entrepreneur or business owner must adapt their thinking to time tested ways of analyzing situations, processing available information and making the right judgments.

Often because of limited resources an entrepreneur may be forced to wear many hats in running a business. This makes it even more important for them to work with the right business mind-set so that they make as few mistakes as possible.

In this chapter I will touch on some of the basic business mind-sets that successful business owners must have to enable them to truly make a success of their business dream.

PROBLEM SOLVING MENTALITY

> Every business solves a problem. It provides a solution to the problems of yesterday, of today, or of tomorrow.

You must first appreciate that every business solves a problem. It provides a solution to the problems of yesterday, of today, or of tomorrow. On a daily basis, businesses are faced with unforeseen problems, often very challenging ones which require immediate attention. As a business owner you must therefore see yourself as a solution provider, ready to add value and inspiration

NEVER ALLOW PROBLEMS TO RUFFLE YOU - THEY ARE OPPORTUNITIES IN DISGUISE.

to what you do and to your customer's lives on a daily basis. **Thomas Edison** once said, *"I never perfected an invention that I did not think about in terms of the service it might give others...I find out what the world needs, then I proceed to invent."*

The key is to never allow the problems to ruffle you because they are opportunities in disguise. Take advantage of them to become a better manager and a successful entrepreneur by addressing them.

EVERY PROBLEM IS AN OPPORTUNITY TO BECOME BETTER, TO KNOW BETTER AND TO DO BETTER.

Always remember that every problem is an opportunity to become better, to know better and to do better.

THE MARK OF A SUCCESSFUL BUSINESSMAN OR WOMAN IS HOW THEY DEAL WITH AND OVERCOME OBSTACLES.

Shy away from problems and you lose the opportunity to test your resolve in managing a business. The mark of a successful businessman or woman is how they deal with and overcome obstacles. Never forget that.

BIGGER PURPOSE/VISION THAN MONEY

As an entrepreneur your business must have a clear, unique, and well-understood vision or purpose and it must be much broader than just making money from your passion. Purpose for a business is seen as the fundamental proposition upon which the organization rests. As **Henry Ford** once said, *"A business that makes nothing but money is a poor business."* In most interviews, successful entrepreneurs often express the fact that they aren't in it for the money. They often speak of higher goals such as the desire to make a positive impact or to contribute to the community, society and the world at large, the love for what they do, or the pursuit of fulfilling an inner sense of worth.

YOUR BUSINESS MUST HAVE A CLEAR, UNIQUE, AND WELL-UNDERSTOOD VISION OR PURPOSE AND IT MUST BE MUCH BROADER THAN JUST MAKING MONEY FROM YOUR PASSION.

It is therefore very important that you clearly establish reasons other than money to be in business. For instance, when employees know the purpose of the organization, they know how their jobs contribute to its success and they are more likely to work together to achieve these goals. Customers, clients, suppliers, regulators, and visitors also get the sense that 'these people know what they are doing'. Having a bigger vision also enables you to 'stick with it' and to continue to work at it, to find better ways of delivering your products and services until you get the right profitable balance. Because without that, it is easy to give up in the face of the smallest challenge or to keep jumping to the next money-making scheme without sticking at a particular idea or business long enough to master it and reap the rewards."

HAVING A BIGGER VISION ALSO ENABLES YOU TO 'STICK WITH IT' AND TO CONTINUE TO WORK AT IT TO FIND BETTER WAYS OF DELIVERING YOUR PRODUCTS AND SERVICES UNTIL YOU GET THE RIGHT PROFITABLE BALANCE

I DON'T KNOW IT ALL

"It takes humility to realize that we don't know everything, not to rest on our laurels and know that we must keep learning and observing. If we don't, we can be sure some startup will be there to take our place."
Cher Wang - CEO, HTC

Another important mentality to settle within yourself is the fact that, no matter how passionate you are about your idea and business, it is simply impossible to know it all. There are so many diverse aspects of business that you must understand in order to maximize the opportunities that come your way from supplier management to marketing, sales, promotions, finance, accounting, customer relationship management, staffing and recruitment.

> NO MATTER HOW PASSIONATE YOU ARE ABOUT YOUR IDEA AND BUSINESS, IT IS SIMPLY IMPOSSIBLE TO KNOW IT ALL.

For instance, let's consider that you are a writer. You may be passionate about writing, however, in your business you will need to know how to negotiate with other service providers (editors, copywriters, publishers, designers, etc.) to bring your manuscript to a publishable standard; marketing professionals to help you market the books; distributors, book stores and other retailers to sell the books. You will need to organize book launches and book signing events, speaking engagements, manage social media and rights and royalties from various sources; all of these elements need to come together to enable you to make a decent living from being a writer.

I have come across quite a number of business owners who have been running their business with limited knowledge of how business functions as a whole. Consider the fact that business is not just about buying and selling but is a whole host of components that need to be applied and balanced to make it all work. Settle that in your mind and you will be on course for greater success in business.

HUMBLE ENOUGH TO ASK FOR HELP

Following from the previous point is the all-important element of humility which is important to cultivate if you don't have it already. From experience I think lack of humility to ask for help is a real problem often disregarded by a significant number of entrepreneurs. With the advent of technology and the internet, reaching out to experts and support systems has never been easier. If we acknowledge that entrepreneurs do not know it all then it is only common sense to agree that they will need help along the way if they want to make a success of the journey and therefore they must ask for it where necessary.

Of course, that does not mean signing up to anyone offering to help. Not every offer of help will be right for you. However, there is so much information available and so many ways to access the best help.

Interestingly, there has never been a better time for governments around the world to appreciate the role of entrepreneurship in the socio-economic development of their economies. Many have set up small business development support units and departments, enacted laws and policies, established entrepreneur hubs, and created all sorts of other support networks and systems to help entrepreneurs and new businesses become successful businesses.

Notwithstanding that, available to most entrepreneurs are a whole host of private business advisory and coaching experts and professionals, like myself, who offer one-on-one professional services, tools such as this book, blogs, daily tips, training seminars etc., to guide and help entrepreneurs to turn their concepts and ideas into thriving and successful businesses. Unfortunately, I have come across many business owners who simply do not acknowledge that they need help, let alone seek out ways to get help or to identify the right kind of help to enable them to avoid costly mistakes associated with 'running blind' in pursuing their dream. In some cases, those who seek help are not receptive to the advice being offered to them. It's your business and you have to make the final call but I wonder why you would look for an expert, verify their expertise, check out their track record, be offered quality advice and then refuse to take on board what has been shared with you. If the reason for refusing to follow through is based on logical analysis, then so be it. However, it is only appropriate to seek help, and when offered that help, take it on board.

Professional experts who can be of great help include business consultants, coaches, mentors, marketing professionals, agents, accountants, brand experts, etc. Most of these professionals will be eager to draw from their expertise, years of professional training, experience, and network of other professionals and resources to help budding business owners and entrepreneurs. They have, most likely, helped other clients with similar challenges and have learnt new and better ways that can help you.

> To succeed in business, you need help. However, you need to acknowledge you need it."

To succeed in business, you need help, and help is available, however, you need to acknowledge you need it, seek the right people to help you and when offered advice, you need to take it on board and act on it.

BUSINESS IS BUILT, NOT INVENTED IN ONE GO

One other way of approaching business is to see it as a building process or as something that needs developing - not an invention. That is why you should not disregard the process but keenly engage in it and commit to it. As with the development of a child you must learn to crawl before attempting to walk, let alone run because you don't just get to take over the world in one go. It is all about taking one market, community, city or nation at a time. Even if you had an instant explosion of your brand, if the basics are not in place and you are not well adapted to the process of growth, over-exposure could crush you and that could be more costly and devastating than you can imagine. When all is said and done, you can invent a thing, but not a business, because business is meant to be developed over time.

> YOU CAN INVENT A THING, BUT NOT A BUSINESS, BECAUSE BUSINESS IS MEANT TO BE DEVELOPED OVER TIME.

SUCCESS IS NOT INSTANT

The prospect of owning a business is exciting especially when you have read or heard about so many successful businesses from the news, books, training seminars, key note speakers etc. However, often there seems to be little appreciation for the fact that no matter how passionate you are about your idea or business, there is nothing like *instant success* in business.

I couldn't agree more with **Katherine Waddell**, host of '*This Needs To Be Said*', TV Show, who said, "it takes 5 to 10 years to be an overnight success."

> FOR EVERY ESTABLISHED BUSINESS THERE IS A STORY BEHIND ITS SUCCESS OR CONTINUED EXISTENCE.

Often by the time we read a success story or listen to an interview, a significant amount of time will have passed from the day the business started to the day it is afforded the opportunity to talk about itself. There is almost certainly very limited time and/or space for the business to share the details of the journey to that point.

> IT IS NAÏVE TO BELIEVE IN 'FOLLOWING YOUR PASSION' WITHOUT MANAGING YOUR EXPECTATIONS ALONG THE WAY.

The headlines never do justice to the full story. Unfortunately, this has, and continues to, deceptively skew the mind of aspiring entrepreneurs and new business owners and leads them to fall into the trap of 'expecting too much too soon'.

Often, new entrepreneurs overlook the fact that for every established business there is a story behind its success or continued existence. These success stories are the result of years of persistence, smart thinking, hard work, fine tuning ideas and systems, near misses of opportunities, errors, and sometimes near bankruptcy experiences. It is therefore naïve to believe in 'following your passion' without managing your expectations along the way.

> **REFUSING TO MANAGE ONE'S EXPECTATION OF THE TIME IT TAKES TO ATTAIN SUCCESS IN BUSINESS IS ONE OF THE MAJOR CAUSES OF BUSINESS FAILURES WITHIN THE FIRST 2-3 YEARS.**

In my experience, refusing to manage one's expectation of the time it takes to attain success in business is one of the major causes of business failures within the first 2-3 years. It is easier to pack up instead of persevering until you get the right balance of making enough to sustain yourself and growing the business successfully.

THE MOST IMPORTANT PEOPLE <u>IN</u> YOUR BUSINESS – YOU AND YOUR EMPLOYEES

"*The distance between number one and number two is always a constant. If you want to improve the organization, you have to improve yourself and the organization gets pulled up with you. That is a big lesson.*" **Indra Nooyi** - Chairperson & CEO, PepsiCo

I couldn't agree more with this quote. It also emphasizes why, as a business owner, you must cultivate the mentality that the success of your business has everything to do with you if you are a one person business, and with you and your employees if you have any. How you evolve with technological advances, changing economic trends, skills development, market knowledge and consumer trends plays a major role in how much you can achieve as a business or how far you can go in business.

Nothing stays static in life, at least not in this fast paced 21st century business environment. Your ability to move with the times can have significant impact on the success of the business.

Often, entrepreneurs are so focused on their idea or their products and services that they don't give due attention to maintaining their relevance in business. However, to grow a successful business you and your employees need access to up to date resources, tools and skills training to thrive. From day one of nursing the idea of going into business, you should start researching, studying and understanding the basics of business which includes identifying specific subjects you have little or no knowledge of which could be relevant to your success.

> **NOTHING STAYS STATIC IN LIFE, AT LEAST NOT IN THIS FAST PACED 21ST CENTURY BUSINESS ENVIRONMENT.**

This is why training and development is an essential part of any successful organization's strategy. Of course, if you work alone you may feel that you must constantly be selling and have no time for training courses, seminars, conferences, industry related trade shows etc. but all of these offer great refresher learning opportunities to enable you and your team to stay at the cutting edge of your industry.

> **TRAINING AND DEVELOPMENT IS AN ESSENTIAL PART OF ANY SUCCESSFUL ORGANIZATION'S STRATEGY**

Even if you have employees, the temptation to overlook this vital aspect of skills training and development is there, especially when business seems to be doing well.

The benefits of investing in yourself and your employees are:

- Makes you relevant to the industry and business environment.
- Opens your eyes to new strategies, trends tools and technology to enable you accomplish more.
- Helps you cut costs by employing new cost saving methods and doing away with outdated tools, methodologies and systems.
- Helps saves time as you learn and adopt new and improved ways of doing things, such as reaching new markets, more efficient service delivery, quicker turnaround times.
- Serves as a huge source of motivation for both yourself and your employees as you experience growth in your personal development. *"Knowledge creates enthusiasm."* **Thomas J. Watson**, Sr.
- Breeds confidence, enabling you and your employees to better serve your target market.
- Gives you a competitive edge because of your breadth of knowledge as well as being up to date with market trends.
- All of which has a huge potential to increase your bottom line or turnover.

As you continue to work on your business, make a conscious commitment to work on yourself and your employees first. This ensures that you are better positioned to serve your clients and customers more efficiently and to deliver excellent service and quality products which is the best way to guarantee success in your business. **Richard Branson**, founder of the Virgin group of companies, once said, *"Clients do not come first. Employees come first. If you take care of your employees, they will take care of the clients."* That, to me, affirms the fact that, yes, the customer is important to the business, however, for the business to best serve the customer, employees are the most important in the business to make it a better organization to serve the customer.

Finally, always remember that *"An investment in knowledge pays the best interest."* **Benjamin Franklin**

THE MOST IMPORTANT PERSON <u>TO</u> YOUR BUSINESS – THE CUSTOMER

> **Y**OU MUST KNOW WHO YOUR CUSTOMERS ARE, UNDERSTAND THEIR NEEDS, AND KNOW HOW TO REACH OUT AND INTERACT WITH THEM.

At the centre of every business activity is a customer or client. That is why it is inconceivable to ignore their needs and wants. The question is, 'who is a customer?'.

A customer is basically the end user of your product or service. It can be a client, buyer, or purchaser of an organization's products or services, an individual, another business, charity or a government organization. Whoever they are, it is very important to clearly establish in your mind that the customer is the most important person to your business.

The customer is:

- Your best friend,
- Your best critique,
- And the most easily available funder/financier.

> **S**UCCESSFUL BUSINESS PEOPLE ARE CUSTOMER-FOCUSED, NOT PRODUCT-FOCUSED AND YOU MUST DO EVERYTHING YOU CAN TO ADAPT TO CHANGING TIMES AND CUSTOMER NEEDS OVER THE LIFETIME OF YOUR BUSINESS.

Sam Walton, the American businessman founder of Walmart and Sam's Club, couldn't have made it any clearer. He said, "*There is only one boss, the customer. And he can fire everybody in the company from the chairman on down, simply by spending his money somewhere else.*" Once they do that, you have no business.

You must know who your customers are, understand their needs, and know how to reach out and interact with them. This is a very important reason why you must be able to clearly define who your target market is right from the start of the business. Business owners often struggle to do this and may assume that everyone is their customer. In my next book, I will talk about the seven types of customers and the strategies to reach out to them and encourage them to do business with you.

Successful business people are customer-focused, not product-focused and you must do everything you can to adapt to changing times and customer needs over the lifetime of your business. "*A brand is not saying what it is, it's what the customer THINKS it is.*" **Karen Katz**, CEO of Neiman Marcus

I**T IS BETTER TO SEE THE CUSTOMER AS 'DOING YOU A FAVOR' BY CHOOSING YOU ABOVE THE COMPETITION AND PATRONIZING YOUR PRODUCTS AND SERVICES RATHER THAN THE OTHER WAY ROUND.**

Your relationship with your customer must be paramount. It is better to see the customer as 'doing you a favor' by choosing you above the competition and patronizing your products and services rather than the other way round. It is also the reason why you must adopt some level of flexibility, whenever possible, in meeting customer needs. Take customer feedback very seriously even if it sounds ridiculous. As Bill Gates once said, "Your most unhappy customers are your greatest source of learning."

It is also worth knowing that an unhappy customer can do a business significant harm. That is why, even in the face of a bad review, your ability to manage it well can turn the customer's bad experience into the beginning of an outstanding new relationship. A customer who is made to feel that they are only important for their cash may be tempted to vote with their feet and go elsewhere. I am sure that as a business owner you have had some form of negative service experience as a customer. How the situation was resolved will have informed your decision to either do business again with the organization or not.

The basic tenets of good customer service are:
- Professionalism should be at the forefront of your thinking when doing business with anyone, including customers and potential customers. It confirms to the customer that they have your respect and that you are serious and know what you are doing.
- Politeness in your dealings with customers. Good manners and courtesy is necessary at all times even when you are entitled to be angry or a customer does not buy anything from you. Basic things like 'hello', 'sir', 'madam', 'good morning', 'thank you very much', 'we are sorry', are very important in winning customers over.
- Personalizing how you address customers goes a long way in earning favor with them as it indicates that you know them and treat them as individuals.
- Promptness in attending to the customer, avoiding delays and cancellations at all cost. And, if needed, follow up with an apology and explanation with the possibility of throwing in a token of goodwill to compensate for any inconvenience to the customer.

Ultimately, every contact your customers have with you and your business is an opportunity for you to cement a lasting reputation with them thus increasing the likelihood of gaining their trust and their repeat business. Providing and delivering high quality, professional, helpful service and assistance before, during and after the customer's needs are met is essential for growing a successful business.

At some point in business, you may have to evaluate the types of clients you have and potentially focus on those who actually bring you the most business. This may mean 'firing' some of them and politely refusing their business especially those who demand so much of your time and resources which you could have channeled to other clients who bring you more income. Bear in mind the 80-20 rule. This is the Pareto principle (the law of the vital few, and the principle of factor sparcity) and states that, for many events, roughly 80% of the effects come from 20% of the causes. In other words, 80% of your business could be coming from 20% of your customers thus the need to focus more on satisfying the needs of these 20% to get more of their business.

> EVERY CONTACT YOUR CUSTOMERS HAVE WITH YOU AND YOUR BUSINESS IS AN OPPORTUNITY FOR YOU TO CEMENT A LASTING REPUTATION WITH THEM

Always remember that it costs more to acquire a new customer than to maintain a satisfied customer. In the words of **Ray Kroc**, *"If you work just for money, you'll never make it, but if you love what you're doing and you always put the customer first, success will be yours."*

Finally, *"Here's the key to success in business. Become obsessed with your customer. Fixate on your customer. Think of the customer. Think of what the customer wants, what the customer needs. What the customer will pay for, what the customer's problems are."* **Brian Tracy**

TAKING CALCULATED RISK

Risk taking is no stranger to entrepreneurship. To start a business is a risk in itself, a leap of faith as some would call it, and always commendable especially if you had to leave a well-established career to become a business owner. Starting a business often means putting your career, personal life, finances and even your health on the line. However, the rewards of entrepreneurship often outweigh these personal risks, that is, if you are prepared to make success of the decision to step out and step up. The potential risks should, however, not be enough to discourage you from pursuing the entrepreneurial dream, rather you should see them as stepping stones to a greater cause and accept that potential risks can help prepare you to better manage them. To succeed in business, you must be prepared for the risks and challenges that come with it.

> To succeed in business, you must be prepared for the risks and challenges that come with it.

As a business owner you will be making decisions on a daily basis, most of which will demand that you make a choice between available options. Some may be quite straight forward, others may present you with less facts to consider with no guarantee of a good outcome. However, not making those choices will either result in inaction or missing potentially lucrative opportunities which is not what you set out to do. Whatever you do, you must always bear in mind that you must take risks but they must be measured or calculated risks. Before making a final decision you must examine all available facts and possibilities within a reasonable time frame and avoid being impulsive or irresponsible.

TIME ON BUSINESS

Time is one of the most expensive resources on earth. In the words of **Peter Drucker**, "*Time is the scarcest resource and unless it is managed nothing else can be managed.*" Time is such that once lost, it is lost forever. It is also one of the greatest assets every human being has been gifted with in equal measure. However, for most of us the 24 hour day is never enough.

Running a business, especially a start-up or new business, can take a lot of time and there is often no limit on the number of hours you could work on your business. How much of your life the business absorbs depends largely on the nature of the business and what you want from it or want to achieve with it. As an entrepreneur seeking to grow a successful business you have to come to terms with the fact that realistically speaking there is a conscious need to sacrifice some of your normal routine activities and leisure time, especially in the early days. This is something that needs to be settled in your mind right from the start to enable you to avoid stressing yourself about all the activities you may be missing out on. You must accept that these short term sacrifices are necessary in order to get the business on the right footing. Once the business picks up and you are able to hire others to help you will be able to gradually restore some, if not all, of the routine activities which you put on hold.

> IT'S NOT HOW MUCH TIME, BUT WHAT YOU DO IN THE TIME THAT MAKES IT MEANINGFUL TO ALL PARTIES.

However, to maintain a good balance between giving as much as you need to and your well-being you need to make time for breaks to avoid impairing your health and to rejuvenate yourself because lack of rest can have a significant impact on your decision making and productivity.

Making quality time for your family must also be factored in. It's not how much time, but what you do in the time that makes it meaningful to all parties. One of the suggested ways of ensuring your family life is not significantly compromised is, where possible, to involve the family even if it's just asking them to help with menial tasks. Often, that helps them to appreciate the process and the demands of your business, as well as offering you the opportunity to connect as you work together.

To ensure you maximize the 24 hour day we all have and establish the best balance, you need to prioritize tasks and plan on a day to day and week by week basis. However, you must always allow flexibility to manage emergencies should there be any in the course of your day or week. Ultimately, your ability to appreciate the demands of running a business and mastering the art of managing your time is a key to being successful, not only in business but in life.

ART OF DELEGATION

Delegation is about entrusting certain functions and tasks to others in the business and holding them accountable to you for the results. This is more than just assigning tasks to subordinates because it gives them the latitude to decide on the means to achieve the set objective and the commensurate authority to be able to carry out the task.

In business, the art of delegation is one many entrepreneurs struggle with. Often they get so emotionally attached to the business idea that it becomes difficult for them to trust others to handle any aspects that

> **D**ELEGATION ALLOWS YOU AND YOUR MANAGEMENT TEAM TO FOCUS ON YOUR PRIMARY FUNCTIONS.

require decisions to be made. For an entrepreneur working alone or with few employees, it is quite common to want to hold on to all the decision making. However, in order to grow you must come to terms with the fact that you need to be able to delegate some responsibilities to others in your team or even to outsource to experts in the industry so that you can focus on other major aspects of running the business. It is one of the smartest ways to expand your business.

Delegation allows you and your management team to focus on your primary functions including planning, organizing, directing, controlling and coordinating. Often the difficulty is that entrepreneurs do not have the presence of mind to fully appreciate this, thus they resort to micromanaging every aspect of the business which can become counterproductive. A good understanding of the benefits of delegation should be convincing enough for the entrepreneur seeking to grow a successful business to learn to delegate in order to focus on the big picture.

Some of the benefits include:

- Helping you as the business owner and other management to focus on the bigger picture by driving the business rather than working in the business
- Helping to bring order to the organization as responsibilities are delegated to staff with expected corresponding accountability.
- Helping to speed up the decision making process thus saving the business significant time in responding to situations, such as taking advantage of opportunities and responding to customer complaints.
- Enabling the business to run smoothly even in the absence of the business owner or other senior management because, except in major issues, employees have the capacity to quickly respond to situations.
- Breeding confidence in staff, leading to improved communication skills.
- Making the team feel more committed and involved in running the business, leading to job satisfaction and staff retention.
- Providing a good training tool for developing leadership and managerial skills among employees as well as a fair assessment basis and a measure of appraising performance.

- Improving team work and team building.
- Giving subordinates space to improve their unique abilities and skills. Managers equally get the opportunity to focus on becoming best at managing.
- Helping inefficiencies to be easily identified because those with delegated authority are more inclined to spot issues at the 'work floor level' and are able to provide relevant feedback to management.
- Inspiring innovation and creativity throughout the organization as employees are accountable for tasks they manage and are tasked with successfully managing a section of the business process.

To effectively delegate aspects of the business or process you must choose the right person with the right skills, motivation and interest in the success of the task and business; clearly explain why you chose them and why you believe they can do it; define the expected successful outcome from the task; let them know of the overall benefit or impact on the organization and for the staff such as their annual appraisal and promotion; make available the resources to enable them to carry out their duties or perform the task; request a plan of action with time limits for your approval indicating how they plan to execute the task; put control systems in place and discuss milestones and how progress will be monitored and deviations from the process addressed; make the policies, regulations, rules and limitations associated with the job or work flow fully understood by the staff before commencement of the task; give the staff adequate authority with the responsibility to enable them to achieve the best result; and finally give them the opportu-

> TO EFFECTIVELY DELEGATE ASPECTS OF THE BUSINESS OR PROCESS YOU MUST CHOOSE THE RIGHT PERSON WITH THE RIGHT SKILLS, MOTIVATION AND INTEREST IN THE SUCCESS OF THE TASK AND BUSINESS.

nity to ask questions and affirm your availability should they require it.

To successfully grow the business I hope you are convinced that delegation is something you must become comfortable with. In the end it will not only help you and senior management to focus on the big picture and stick with what you do best but it will also breed confidence in your staff and help them to become acquainted with the responsibilities of managing a business, encouraging them to accept more responsibilities in the future. It is simply one of the best ways to get things done efficiently and effectively within a reasonable time to ensure higher productivity and return on investment.

VALUE PERSPECTIVE

There is a trap I commonly find entrepreneurs fall into, especially new business owners. It is assessing things based only on price or cost. This is something I consider limiting for any business owner seeking to be in business for the long term. From the pricing of products or services to hiring employees to competing in business, value or perceived value has proven to be one of the best ways to measure the true worth of anything.

The truth is that what you sell must be good value if it is going to be the customers' preferred choice over what exists in the market because, most times, customers may not be fully aware of the true cost of production of the items they buy. They are therefore often willing to pay a price based on their perception of how much the product is worth to them and it is up to you to employ marketing strategies to create the right perceived value of the product to sell to them.

Value also helps you to prioritize, assigning different values to different activities. Assigning value to each task enables you to better assess what to take on board, what to delegate and even the order in which each task is to be dealt with.

The question is, what is value or perceived value? The Oxford Advanced Learner's Dictionary defines value as a noun to simply mean "how much something is worth" or "the regard that something is held to deserve; the importance, worth, or usefulness of something." It is therefore a person's opinion of a product's value to them, with little or nothing to do with the price per se but how the product satisfies their need.

Assessing the true value of anything will therefore mean looking beyond what it cost you or the price you paid for it in monetary terms. The challenge is, if you are not able to measure the actual value in monetary terms, then how do you measure it? This is where you have to think about its importance, worth, or usefulness beyond the price being paid for it. For instance, if you hire an employee, you have to be careful not to just look at the expected salary as a measure of their worth. Their experience, the depth and breadth of their know how, how much their contribution will save the business, or how much their presence will add to the business, all come into play.

Another example arises when considering the option of handling your marketing in-house versus hiring a marketing expert or even a business coach to help you drive your business strategy. There is the temptation to only weigh up how much each is costing you in monetary terms when making a decision. However, when you look beyond the cost and start to weigh in factors as an expert's expertise, years of experience, scope of knowledge and industry, qualifications, results from past clients, personality, how easy you connect and can work with them, and how much time and cost of making mistakes via trial and error they will save you there is a much wider scope to assess the true worth of expert help.

Again, it is better to build a business with the aim of delivering value because there is no end to what the business can do to improve on its delivery or offering. It is therefore important to focus on creating more value for your customers and clients. It is a better way to stay ahead by looking for ways of competing in the market place other than lowering price.

> **M**EASURING SUCCESS BY HOW MUCH PROFIT YOU MAKE CAN BE MISLEADING.

Value is also a better measure of ROI than cost: profit ratios or margins. Measuring success by how much profit you make can be misleading as it may lead to you losing sight of all the other non-quantifiable financial benefits of the business such as customer perception of your products and services as well as the business as a whole. This often has a greater impact on long term business performance and survival than immediate financial gains.

Value also gives you more options to carve out a niche for yourself thus offering you a better set of tools to employ in distinguishing yourself from the competition and making

> **V**ALUE ALSO GIVES YOU MORE OPTIONS TO CARVE OUT A NICHE FOR YOURSELF.

you more appealing to your target market. Thankfully it is almost always possible to find something that can be value-added to your products or services. To compete only on price is again not always the smartest strategy, especially in the long term because it can affect

> **T**O COMPETE ONLY ON PRICE IS AGAIN NOT ALWAYS THE SMARTEST STRATEGY, ESPECIALLY IN THE LONG TERM BECAUSE IT CAN AFFECT YOUR MARGINS SIGNIFICANTLY

your margins significantly as you simply cannot continue to drive down prices below a certain point and still make the level of profit that will enable you to remain in business.

There is always something that is important to your clients and customers that you can offer other than cutting prices or offering them discounts. These can include:free and faster delivery;

- making your business much more accessible and more convenient to customers;
- offering better quality products and services;
- speedy and creative ways to respond to customer complaints;
- bundling packages that add significant benefits to the products you are selling;

> **A**SSESSING THE WORTH OF YOUR PRODUCT OR SERVICE ON THE BASIS OF VALUE PROVES TO BE MUCH MORE WHOLESOME THAN USING THE COST OR PRICE OF THE ITEM

- offering more information to help customers make better choices;
- going out of your way to help customers to research a product you do not trade in;
- offering different service package levels (such as gold, platinum, silver packages) for your customers based on frequency of doing business with you, amount of purchase, etc.;
- offering more valuable service, pricing, benefits and related items to customers based on the number of times they buy from you, such as frequent flyer air miles offered by airlines;
- reward systems based on recognizing customers for being outstanding customers over a period, usage of products or services, purchase of certain levels of orders;
- assigning dedicated personnel to manage customers' accounts personally and to provide support;

- providing up to date industry information, tips and other benefits via newsletters.

The fact is that with creativity, innovation and a desire to always stand out and be ahead of the competition there are many things you can do to add value to your product and service delivery.

In summary, assessing the worth of your product or service on the basis of value proves to be much more wholesome than using the cost or price of the item. Not only that, it also offers more options to you in differentiating yourself from competitors and helps you to make better decisions when purchasing products and services for the business.

BRANDING THE BUSINESS

A brand as defined by **The American Marketing Association (AMA)** is a "*name, term, sign, symbol or design, or a combination of them intended to identify the goods and services of one seller or group of sellers and to differentiate them from those of other sellers.*" A brand is therefore a name used to identify and distinguish a specific product, service, or business. It can also be defined as the image of the product in the market. Or it can simply mean your promise to your customers, telling them what they can expect from your business and is the sum of their experiences and perceptions of you and your business overall. Your brand must differentiate you from what your competitors are offering. **Karen Katz**, CEO of Neiman Marcus, defines it as, "*A brand is not saying what it is, it's what the customer THINKS it is.*"

> **Y**OUR BRAND MUST DIFFERENTIATE YOU FROM WHAT YOUR COMPETITORS ARE OFFERING.

Thus branding is "*The process involved in creating a unique name and image for a product in the consumers' mind, mainly through advertising campaigns with a consistent theme. Branding aims to establish a significant and differentiated presence in the market that attracts and retains loyal customers."* - **Online Business Dictionary**

IF BRANDING IS A PROCESS, THEN IT STANDS TO REASON THAT THERE MUST BE A POINT WHERE THE PROCESS IS INITIATED.

If branding is a process, then it stands to reason that there must be a point where the process is initiated. Unfortunately, most entrepreneurs start their business with nothing like this in mind. Often when I ask clients, initial reactions tend to be to shrug it off. Some may say something like, "What has that got to do with this, my small business?".

Let's face it, Nike, Microsoft, Apple, KFC, McDonalds, Ford, Coca-Cola, Toyota, Mercedes, Walmart, Tesco, BP, Shell, and the many other established brands out there, started as a small backyard, table top or garage business.

Engagement in the process starts in the business owner's mind, where all decisions and ideas originate. As a business you must focus on getting your prospects to see you as the only one who provides a solution to their problem and not just about getting your target market to choose you over the competition. Brand strategist Kerry Light once said, "The primary focus of your brand message must be on how special you are, not how cheap you are. The goal must be to sell the distinctive quality of the brand."

BUILDING A BRAND IS LIKE BUILDING A CITY. **A** CITY HAS A NETWORK OF COMPONENTS SUCH AS ROADS, HOUSES, LIBRARIES, AND SHOPPING CENTRES, SO DOES A BRAND.

Building a brand is like building a city. A city has a network of components such as roads, houses, libraries, and shopping centres, so does a brand. Each of the components has its own unique network but still has to fit into the ultimate plan to make the city complete. A city is planned and not built in a day. It's built one component, one day at a time. So is a brand.

A good brand, among other things must:
- Clarify your position in the business.
- Clearly deliver your message.
- Motivate your buyers and deliver on your brand promise.
- Consistently reinforce your identity.
- Confirm your credibility.
- Connect to your target potential emotionally.
- Create loyalty and enthusiasm among your consumers.

> CONSISTENCY, BOTH VISUALLY AND VERBALLY, IS THE KEY IN CREATING A STRATEGIC BRAND.

An established brand, over time, brings with it a host of benefits such as:
- Adding value to your business.
- Developing a loyalty base that cuts costs on marketing and advertising.
- Increase in your turnover.
- Projecting an image of quality in your business.
- Projecting an image of a large and established business that has also been around long enough to be well known.
- Allowing you to link together several different products in your business. As you put your brand name on every product and service you sell, customers for one product will be more likely to buy one of your other products.

Your logo is the starting point in the branding process. The logo must be integrated with your website, social media pages, promotional materials, and packaging to project the kind of image or perception you desire to communicate to your potential customers. Consistency, both visually and verbally, is the key in creating a strategic brand. This often leads to what is commonly referred to as brand equity, the added value your business attracts enabling you to charge more than similar unbranded products in the market could command.

> **B**RAND EQUITY, THE ADDED VALUE YOUR BUSINESS ATTRACTS ENABLING YOU TO CHARGE MORE THAN SIMILAR UNBRANDED PRODUCTS IN THE MARKET COULD COMMAND.

A few of the areas to focus on from day 1 to enable you to at least start the process right include:

- **A memorable and easy-to-remember name** - A good brand name should instinctively be easy to pronounce, attract attention, be easy to remember, be easy to recognize, suggest product benefits and usage, suggest the company or product image, be attractive, stand out among a group of other brands, distinguish the product's positioning in relation to the competition, and be protectable under trademark law. As the **Lexicon** states, *"A brand name is more than a word. It is the beginning of a conversation."*
- **A professionally designed distinctive logo** - Symbols and images are much more noticeable than text. **Diane Ackerman** stated, *"The visual image is a kind of tripwire for the emotions."* The image size, quality, and colors deserve important consideration. Note that every color has a meaning so research various colors and choose the one or combination that best represents your business.

- **A catchy phrase or slogan** - A short but catchy statement that represents your aspiration which customers and potential customers can identify you with and remember.
- **Professionally designed stationery** - This includes business cards, letterhead, websites, social media banners, and brochures. However, it is in using them consistently that will get people associating with your brand.
- **Strategic advertising** - Use social media platforms and tools (most of which are free) until you have funds to pay for advertising in local and national newspapers, radio, television, or use web-based ads such as Google Adwords, Facebook ad, Twitter ad, public relations.

As a small or new business, you may not have enough money to embark on all these right from the start. However, the purpose at this stage is to bear all these factors in mind so that you do not do any one thing for the sake of it. For instance, there are a lot of free business card offers on the Internet. However, the quality of the materials are mostly below standard. A little search-and-spend will get you a professionally designed quality logo, business card, and letterhead, often offered as a complete package which communicates value and seriousness to potential businesses and clients. Also understand that "*a brand is a living entity—and it is enriched or undermined cumulatively over time, the product of a thousand small gestures.*" **Michael Eisner**, Disney - CEO

There are so many aspects of branding that we can talk about under brand management. However, the most important thing to bear in mind is that branding is an ongoing thing and the benefits are enormous if you approach it in the right way as you work your way through the early stages of your business journey.

In conclusion, do all you can to be distinctive and keep repeating your message, be consistent, be persistent, evolve with the times as much as is necessary, stand for something, and be linked with something specific in the minds of your consumers, and protect your distinction.

PROTECT YOUR IDENTITY

Closely related to branding is the need to protect your business identity, including your inventions, unique symbols, designs, logos, concepts or a combination of these. There is no wisdom in spending time and resources to build a brand only to realize that someone else who arrived on the scene later has formally protected the name or logo or concept first. Bear in mind that the regulation for securing the intellectual property rights leans towards the first person who takes the steps to submit a formal application. The process and type of protection differs from nation to nation. For instance, in the UK trademarking a name, logo or unique symbol can take an average of 4-6 months so it is worth making the necessary inquiries as soon as possible, especially to find out if what you seek to protect can be formally protected or not.

A trademark will give a business an exclusive right to use the logo design or symbol, and may lawfully prosecute any parties that use the same trademark in the future. For a business name to be trademarked in most jurisdictions or countries it may have to be established through actual use in the marketplace or through registration of the mark with the trademarks office or trademarks registry in that country or jurisdiction. However, in some jurisdictions trademark rights may be established through either or both means. Please note, registering a company name with the body responsible for registering of a business in most countries, be it Companies House in the UK, Federal States Business Entity Registration Offices in the USA, Registrar of Companies in (ROC) in India, Registrar of Companies - also known as CIPRO in South Africa, Office of the Registrar General in Ghana or The Corporate Affairs Commission of Nigeria etc, does not necessarily mean that you have a trademark of your company name even though no other business can be registered as your name.

> **TO MASTER BUSINESS IS TO MASTER THE WAY SUCCESSFUL BUSINESS PEOPLE THINK.**

In summary, we can see that the mind-set of an entrepreneur is as important as the business idea itself and the success of the business is directly linked to it. What is important is that, as an entrepreneur, you must "*make your mind-set a top priority because the actions you take (or don't take) always stems from your thoughts.*" **Kathleen Deggelman**. To master business is to master the way successful business people think and how they apply the above factors in running their business. "*Success or failure in business is caused more by the mental attitude even than by mental capacities.*" **Walter Scott**

Having the right mind-set for business is simply non-negotiable because it is the foundation to everything else you will have to do to run the business successfully on a daily basis. Never lose sight of that fact.

> **THE MIND-SET OF AN ENTREPRENEUR IS AS IMPORTANT AS THE BUSINESS IDEA ITSELF AND THE SUCCESS OF THE BUSINESS IS DIRECTLY LINKED TO IT.**

In the next chapter we will talk about another vital skill needed to add to your passion and enhance your ultimate success in business: negotiation skills.

> **HAVING THE RIGHT MIND-SET FOR BUSINESS IS SIMPLY NON-NEGOTIABLE BECAUSE IT IS THE FOUNDATION TO EVERYTHING ELSE YOU WILL HAVE TO DO TO RUN A SUCCESSFUL BUSINESS.**

CHAPTER 8

PASSION GIVES YOU THE IDEA, BUT DO YOU KNOW HOW TO GET THE BEST FROM NEGOTIATIONS?

"In Business As in Life, You Don't Get What You Deserve, You Get What You Negotiate." **Chester L. Karrass**

Negotiation skills are essential skills every entrepreneur must have. They are critical to your success in business and can be the difference between success or failure. Developing good negotiation skills must therefore be a priority for you as a business owner. These are skills that you will rely on from day one of being in business and from informal day-to-day interactions to processing formal transactions, internally and externally, negotiating skills will be needed in your dealings with:

- services providers (e.g. graphic designers, business coaches and consultants, marketing agencies, etc.)
- potential partners
- customers
- creditors
- debtors
- suppliers
- employees
- investors
- banks

- tax authorities
- regulators
- government agencies

You will negotiate on issues such as conditions of sale, wage packages, leases, service delivery and other legal contracts including resolving customer complaints. In other words, almost every business transaction or relationship has to be negotiated to get a deal signed, an agreement in place or an understanding reached. It is vital to have the mind-set that everything is negotiable in business.

HAVE THE MIND-SET THAT EVERYTHING IS NEGOTIABLE IN BUSINESS.

It also stands to reason that, "*In business, you don't get what you deserve, you get what you negotiate for.*" **Chester Karrass**

Poor negotiation skills can cost you significantly from losing strategic customers to vital business partnerships.

The Business Dictionary defines negotiation as " *Bargaining (give and take) process between two or more parties (each with its own aims, needs, and viewpoints) seeking to discover a common ground and reach an agreement to settle a matter of mutual concern or resolve a conflict.*" It can also be defined as a process where two or more parties with different needs and goals discuss an issue to find an acceptable solution mutually beneficial to both parties.

A SUCCESSFUL NEGOTIATION IS ACHIEVED WHEN YOU MAKE ALLOWANCES FOR THINGS THAT MAY MEAN LITTLE TO YOU WHILE GIVING SOMETHING TO THE OTHER PARTY THAT MEANS A LOT TO THEM.

Negotiations usually require some form of give and take. The aim should not always be to win or to be right because sometimes building relationships for the long term is more important than creating an entrenched stance. The objective should always be to remain courteous and constructive throughout the process to arrive at a point that delivers a win-win situation for both parties. Regardless of any differences in each party's interest, the approach must be aimed at fostering goodwill in the end. Psychology plays a significant role in negotiations. The key is to be well prepared on the object of the negotiations as well as the parties involved.Often a successful negotiation is achieved when you make allowances for things that may mean little to you while giving something to the other party that means a lot to them. A good negotiation therefore leaves each party satisfied and ready to do business again and again. Negotiation therefore has the capacity to help foster a healthy and long lasting relationship.

Howard Baker once said, "*the most difficult thing in any negotiation, almost, is making sure that you strip it of the emotion and deal with the facts.*"

Effective communication is vital to the success of any negotiation. You must master verbal, non-verbal and written language. A good negotiator is able to decipher between what is said, written or not said, and what is meant. Where there is the slightest hint of ambiguity, clarification is sought to ensure both parties are on the 'same page'.

> A GOOD NEGOTIATOR IS ABLE TO DECIPHER BETWEEN WHAT IS SAID, WRITTEN OR NOT SAID, AND WHAT IS MEANT.

That said, a good negotiator must:
- Be honest and respectful at all times.
- Genuinely show interest, and pay attention, using body language or brief verbal replies that show interest and concern in the process.
- Be an effective listener by allowing the other party to do most of the talking. Apply the 70/30 rule here. Listen 70 percent of the time and talk only 30 percent of the time. Encourage other parties to talk by asking

more open-ended questions which are questions that can't be answered with a simple "yes" or "no." In effect, be a good communicator, employing effective communication skills including positive body language.

- Ask as many questions as necessary throughout the process and let the other party or parties know you heard them. Summarize what they have said because this helps to confirm that what you heard is what they actually meant.
- Write proceedings down whilst paying attention to as many details as possible.
- Be well prepared and know their strengths or advantage, if any, such as expertise, skills, experience, reputation, scope, etc.
- Have a clear understanding of who the other parties are, because the best way of getting what you want is to focus on what the other party needs. Know what they specifically want and what other options are available to them, what they are bringing to the table and what their basic interests and expectations are.
- Be creative and seek to work together for a mutually beneficial solution.
- Draw a clear line between negotiables and non-negotiables.
- Be flexible and prepared for compromise along the way. Compromise must be based on the negotiables and be around shared interests. Never give anything away without getting something in return for it.
- Be clear and consistent on the goals and objectives of the negotiations. Be optimistic, aim high and expect the best outcome but at the same time be realistic.
- Avoid distraction from minor issues and always keep your mind on the big picture, knowing what issues are

to be formally negotiated and what are minor issues to be addressed.

- Be interested in reaching a win-win outcome. Often, the 'take it or leave it' attitude does not give room for a successful negotiation and as such is not a good approach.
- Establish guidelines for the negotiation process and work together to stick with them.
- Where necessary, seek legal advice to establish terms.
- Focus on value in your assessment and considerations rather than just the numbers, by way of cost or asking price to be paid, etc.
- Always consider both the short term and long term potential of any collaboration with the other party that could stem from the relationship.
- Be professional, patient and remain calm each step of the way, avoiding any form of confrontation.
- Focus on the issue and avoid becoming personal, angry, frustrated or even hostile at any point.
- If the other party or parties are people of other cultures and nationalities, be sensitive to cultural differences. Expectations, language, perceptions and processes must be duly factored in as you engage them in the negotiations.
- Avoid rushing to sign a deal. Never allow yourself to be put under pressure. Gain time and space to think it over, especially if it's a long term deal or one with a large price tag or significant consequences should anything go wrong.
- Ensure that your team's goals (if working as a team) and your client's needs are aligned and all parties in your team with decision making capacity agree to the terms with the other party before anything is signed.

- Avoid blaming the other party in the event of a dispute or inability to achieve a deal.
- Exhaust all possibilities that meet your shared interests before giving up on the negotiations.
- Give yourself the option to walk away if the deal is not satisfactory to you. This mentality often sends a signal to the other party that you are serious and forces them to make some concessions in your favor. Without this mentality you may look desperate or vulnerable and you may be inclined to give in to the other party's demands just to get a deal signed.

The ability of an entrepreneur to master this all-important skill is too important to ignore because the outcome of good negotiations contributes significantly to the success of every aspect of your business, including:

- It helps bring clarity to the nature of business relationships you enter into with external parties enabling you to build better relationships as you both have a full understanding of what each party is bringing to the table and the expectations of each other.
- It allows you to build, maintain and become better at workplace relationships enabling you to better manage the business.
- It offers parties clear guidelines in pursuit of the object of the business relationship.
- It enables you to become more efficient in business as you are able to avoid hours of potential arguments when trying to get others on board with an idea or project because of your ability to negotiate skilfully and effectively.
- It helps you to focus on other aspects of the business after a deal has been signed, knowing that a clear

working understanding is in place to manage the way forward.

- It ensures that parties have clear responsibilities and are accountable to each other for execution.
- It helps you to avoid future problems and conflicts as well as providing something to refer to in the event of a dispute.
- It ensures employees are fully informed and aware of the direction management is taking the organization after a deal is signed.
- Training of staff in negotiation skills significantly benefits the business in other areas due to the transferability of these skills and their applicability in all areas of the business.
- Good negotiation skills enable you to save significant amounts of money for your business when negotiating with suppliers especially on bulk or large purchases, contractors and other service providers and agencies.
- It enables you to make more money by being able to negotiate your way by getting the best selling price from buyers and customers.
- It enables you to secure long term business collaborations and partnerships that can significantly impact your profitability and long term success in business.

From the above it is evident that developing negotiation skills is non-negotiable for entrepreneurs and business owners. Negotiation can be learned and the skill can be improved on over time and with practice. It is one skill that the success of your business hangs on from the first steps you take to bring your idea to reality.

NEGOTIATION CAN BE LEARNED AND THE SKILL CAN BE IMPROVED ON OVER TIME AND WITH PRACTICE.

CHAPTER 9

PASSION GIVES YOU THE IDEA, BUT DO YOU HAVE A STRATEGY IN PLACE TO GROW THE BUSINESS?

"Sound strategy starts with having the right goal….. Strategy is about making choices, trade-offs; it's about deliberately choosing to be different…. The company without a strategy is willing to try anything." **Michael Porter**, Professor at Harvard Business School, and a leading authority on company strategy and the competitiveness of nations and regions

A strategy is simply an *'elaborate and systematic plan of action.'* – WordNet Dictionary. A business strategy therefore is simply the means by which the business sets out to achieve its desired objectives. It can also be described as the way in which a company addresses or deals with its ongoing opportunities and challenges to become more successful.

The truth is that, in business, unless you have a carefully crafted business strategy, you are simply operating by trial and error. An American professional baseball catcher, manager, and coach, **Lawrence Peter "Yogi" Berra**, once said, *"If you don't know where you are going, you will likely end up somewhere else."* That said, you

> IN BUSINESS, UNLESS YOU HAVE A CAREFULLY CRAFTED BUSINESS STRATEGY, YOU ARE SIMPLY OPERATING BY TRIAL AND ERROR.

can have a business plan but without a clear cut strategy to execute it, it will remain sketchy and difficult to follow. Irrespective of how passionate you are about the business, taking the time to craft a good strategy is a must for your business success.

A business strategy can cover periods of 1-3 years, 3-5 years, or even 5-10 years, although most organizations these days focus on shorter periods in developing strategies for their business due to the fast pace of change in the business environment and the global economy.

A business strategy can also focus on specific aspects of the business, such as, a project, how to effectively allocate resources to segments of the business, how to penetrate a particular market or compete effectively.

There are two main categories of strategies often pursued by business organizations:

1. Generic strategies
    i. Growth and expansion strategies involving developing new products, going into new lines of business, buying new businesses and major assets in order to expand the business.
    ii. Going international or global with the business by expanding into other countries or nations or economic regions.
    iii. Focusing on the most productive and profitable lines, thus cutting back on products and services that are less profitable allowing you to concentrate on what you do best to maximize return on investment.
2. Competitive strategies – these are largely focussed on doing things better than your competitors and not just copying what they are doing. A business owner can do this by:

i. Differentiating yourself from the competition, which can enable you to charge more for your products and services. This is a great way to compete if you concentrate on delivering value rather than just selling to your customer or client. This could mean making your product different from that of your competitors through additional features, packaging and labelling and customer care.

ii. Taking advantage of size and economies of scale to sell your products and services at a lower price than your competitors, especially if you are the market leader.

For a new business, formulating a business strategy can be quite straightforward depending on the industry, trend and nature of the business, as well as where the business wants to position itself, for example as a market leader, at the premium end or as a discount business.

However, for an existing business, it is essential to start with reviewing the organization's past performance, anticipating its future performance in line with its objectives, and designing a strategy that offers the business a road map to help it achieve its desired goals.

A WELL-CRAFTED BUSINESS STRATEGY CLEARLY HELPS YOU TO ARTICULATE THE DIRECTION A BUSINESS WILL PURSUE AND THE STEPS IT WILL TAKE TO ACHIEVE THESE GOALS.

From the above we can see that a well-crafted business strategy clearly helps you to articulate the direction a business will pursue and the steps it will take to achieve these goals. Crafting a better strategy helps a business to establish a clear framework for subsequent decisions giving the business an edge in the marketplace right from the start.

Your understanding of these strategies will help you to choose the winning approach to success.

Before we proceed any further, let us look at the importance or benefits of having a good business strategy.

- It helps the organization to focus on what is most important to its goals, such as, the market that has the most potential to be successful or profitable.
- It helps the business avoid costly mistakes and missed opportunities as management spend time analyzing all options and possibilities when crafting the strategy.
- It serves as a road map to guide management in the business.
- It offers management the opportunity to better adapt to the changing business environment and to respond quickly to take advantage of potential opportunities or to minimize the exposure of the organization to potential losses.
- It helps the business to retain customers and gain repeat customer business through clearly laid out customer care strategies with well-defined guidelines in managing this vital relationship.
- It ensures efficient use of the company's resources, such as raw materials, personnel, time, and logistics.
- It enables the business to discover new business opportunities and markets which would otherwise have been overlooked if effort was not made to formulate a strategy.
- It is also the means by which expansion programs can be effectively executed. Without it, opportunities for expansion can be missed or the business could find itself in a position of being ill prepared to effectively manage expansion.

- It helps to clearly differentiate a business from its competitors, enabling it to compete effectively by being responsive to changing trends and customer needs.
- It enables a business owner to make more logical, confident decisions.
- Ultimately, it is necessary for the achievement of the objectives of the business.

A good strategy must be clearly understood by all parties, used as a guide in the day to day running of the business and must form the basis of all management decisions. Ultimately, it defines the nature, direction and value system of the business as an entity.

> **A GOOD STRATEGY DEFINES THE NATURE, DIRECTION AND VALUE SYSTEM OF THE BUSINESS AS AN ENTITY.**

To formulate the right strategy as a business, the entrepreneur or management must consider factors, such as:

- What are our core values and beliefs as a business?
- What markets and customer groups are we looking to serve?
- What products and services will we offer and how profitable is each one potentially going to be?
- What competitive advantages will cause us to become more profitable and successful?
- What core competencies must we have or improve on to fuel our desired growth?
- How will we market our products and services to our target market?
- How will we sell our products and services to this market?
- What infrastructure, core processes and resources must we have to succeed in the industry?

- What financial results are we looking to achieve, in both the short, medium and long term?

It is important to also understand that having a good strategy is only one side of the story. You require a workable plan to implement it because without that it will be a job half done. Among some of the factors that can stand between a strategy and its implementation are:

- The lack of understanding of the strategy by the team or employees who are often at the forefront of its implementation, if you have employees or working with a team.

A WELL-CRAFTED BUSINESS STRATEGY WITH THE RIGHT IMPLEMENTATION PLAN CAN MAKE A HUGE DIFFERENCE IN AN ORGANIZATION'S QUEST TO GROW AND TO BECOME MORE PROFITABLE AND SUCCESSFUL

- Weak execution of the strategy either due to the above point or lack of commitment to the process. This often happens because employees may comply rather than being totally committed to the goals of the organization.
- If the organization as a whole is not committed to change, implementation may be a struggle, especially where change is required.
- Lack of discipline to ensure a systematic approach to the implementation process.
- It is equally important to know how to bridge the gap between knowing what to do, and actually doing it. The organization can be caught up in talking rather than getting on with the necessary action to implement the actual strategy. For instance, if the implementation process is badly designed or too complex to follow, or management do not have the trust of the employees or the rest of the team, it can become a major barrier to the actual implementation.

In conclusion, a well-crafted business strategy with the right implementation plan can make a huge difference in an organization's quest to grow and to become more profitable and successful, especially if the above limitations are addressed.

Before we end this chapter let me highlight a few areas a business can focus its core strategies on.

MARKETING STRATEGY

Marketing is essentially about getting the right products or services in front of the people who want to buy them. According to the BusinessDictionary.com a marketing strategy is '*an organization's strategy that combines all of its marketing goals into one comprehensive plan.*' In effect, a marketing strategy helps you identify and communicate the benefits of your business to

> A MARKETING STRATEGY HELPS YOU IDENTIFY AND COMMUNICATE THE BENEFITS OF YOUR BUSINESS TO YOUR TARGET MARKET.
>
> A MARKETING PLAN HELPS YOU TO SIMPLY IMPLEMENT YOUR MARKETING STRATEGY

your target market. A marketing plan helps you to simply implement your marketing strategy. A good marketing strategy should also help you focus on the right product mix in order to achieve the maximum profit potential to sustain the business whilst addressing the specific needs of different customer groups. The marketing strategy is the foundation of a marketing plan.

Contents of the marketing strategy should be measurable and actionable and differentiate your company and products from the competition. The objectives of your marketing strategy should also establish specific goals, such as, "*Our goal is to capture 20 percent of the existing market in the next twelve months and 30 percent by the end of three years in ten cities,*" or, "*We want to achieve a turnover of $5 million in the next two years within the southwest region.*"

It must also take into account how your business strengths and weaknesses will affect your marketing.

> **THE MARKETING STRATEGY IS THE FOUNDATION OF A MARKETING PLAN.**

A workable strategy should help you to identify the specific customer segments you are targeting and your positioning in those market segments; identify how to serve your targeted customer segment or group, i.e. define the benefits they are looking for and how you intend to meet them and the technology you intend to use; establish your marketing objectives such as your intended market share, growth, how you intend to enter the market and how you intend to increase awareness of what you are offering; and work out what mix of marketing tools such as products, price, place, and promotion you will use to deliver the benefits to your customers and beat the competition.

> **YOUR MARKETING STRATEGY CAN ONLY BENEFIT YOUR BUSINESS STRATEGY … IF YOU USE IT.**

At the end of the day your marketing strategy can only benefit your business strategy … if you use it.

PRICING STRATEGY

A pricing strategy involves a set of '*activities aimed at finding a product's optimum price, typically including overall marketing objectives, consumer demand, product attributes, competitors' pricing, and market and economic trends.*' – Business Dictionary

Pricing strategies are sometimes not given much consideration by new businesses. Most existing businesses on the other hand tend to stick with the same pricing strategy with little flexibility. However, a pricing strategy is a major determining factor in the survival or success of a business and a workable component of a good marketing strategy. Understanding this and getting it right will positively affect your revenues and profit. For some businesses it's simply looking at what is being charged by competitors and setting prices accordingly. A lower or higher price can significantly change both sales volumes and gross margins and, subsequently, profits.

Understanding some of the factors that influence how much people are willing to pay for goods and services is very important to help you design the right strategy for your products and services. People generally pay a price based on the:

A PRICING STRATEGY IS A MAJOR DETERMINING FACTOR IN THE SURVIVAL OR SUCCESS OF A BUSINESS AND A WORKABLE COMPONENT OF A GOOD MARKETING STRATEGY

- price of substitute products or services in the marketplace;
- price of related products or services available;
- cost of the problem a product or service solves;
- status associated with using or owning such a product or service;
- cost of a problem the product or service prevents;
- location where the product or service is provided;
- persons using the product or service;
- revenues that can be generated from owning the product or service;
- customer service and support provided both before and after the service or product is sold;
- guaranteed warranty period.

Establishing your pricing objectives is undoubtedly among the most basic and important things to do. Other factors such as the cost of production, position in the market, demand of the product or service and environmental factors must also be taken into consideration in designing a pricing strategy.

Ultimately, a good pricing strategy requires a good market research. Find people who will be potential customers of your products, understand their needs and provide what will meet their needs. Settle that and determine your price based on your pricing objectives to ensure the growth and profitability of your business. It is equally important to add value to your products as much as possible instead of relying solely on pricing to make your product more competitive.

ADVERTISING STRATEGY

An advertising strategy is '*a campaign developed by a business to encourage potential customers to purchase goods or services.*' - Business Dictionary

Every business needs to promote itself constantly to reach out to its customers and potential customers. "*Nothing except the mint can make money without advertising.*" **Thomas B. Macaulay**

Advertising is basically the method used by a business to publicize and position its products and services to its target market. It includes elements such as perceived demographics of the audience; geographic location; price points; the use of salespeople, product launches, brand name and image; advertising media such as billboards, websites, or television; promotion of the product in retail and wholesale outlets; press releases and other public relations activities; and special offers.

AN ADVERTISING STRATEGY MUST SUPPORT YOUR MARKETING STRATEGY. THE AIM IS TO ATTRACT THE CUSTOMER, CAPTURE HIS OR HER ATTENTION AND LEAVE AN IMPRESSION OF INTEREST AND SOME LEVEL OF CURIOSITY.

An advertising strategy must support your marketing strategy. The aim is to attract the customer, capture his or her attention and leave an impression of interest and some level of curiosity.

"Good advertising does not just circulate information. It penetrates the public mind with desires and belief." **Leo Burnett** - an American advertising executive and the founder of the Leo Burnett Company.

Advertising may be the only way customers form their first impressions of your business until they ever buy from you so you must use creative strategies to create slogans, sounds, and impressions that will communicate the information you want to send to your intended audience.

"Advertising says to people, 'Here's what we've got. Here's what it will do for you. Here's how to get it'." **Leo Burnett**

> ADVERTISING MAY BE THE ONLY WAY CUSTOMERS FORM THEIR FIRST IMPRESSIONS OF YOUR BUSINESS UNTIL THEY EVER BUY FROM YOU

Bear with me for a moment and consider this. As we embark on our daily routines, we see or hear something being advertised. It gets our attention and, if it's of relevance to us, we become interested. If it has a resemblance to something we need or have been thinking about, what do we do? We desire it and even plan how we will own and use it.

A good advertisement should, therefore:

- Generate awareness of your business.
- Provide basic information on your business contact details.
- Result in increased sales by letting your potential customers know about your product or services.

- Inform customers about latest offers, new product launches, and improvements to your services and products.
- Make you stand out, creating a distinctive brand for your business and establishing you as the first choice for customers.
- Enable you to develop a unique position and niche in the market.
- Be attractive enough to cause suppliers to want to do business with you and even entice potential employees.

> YOU ADVERTISE TO INTRODUCE YOUR PRODUCT OR SERVICE BUT THE QUALITY OF YOUR PRODUCT IS WHAT BRINGS THE RETURNS.

A well-planned advertisement will have long range benefits for any small or new business. To be effective with your advertising strategy, you need to consciously plan for it, choose the best methods or media, and constantly assess the effectiveness of each one. You advertise to introduce your product or service but the quality of your product is what brings the returns. In the final analysis, as **Jef I. Richards** says, "*Advertising is totally unnecessary. Unless you hope to make money.*"

SALES STRATEGY

A sales strategy sets out in detail a plan on how an individual or a business goes about getting its product or service in front of people who need it.

As a new or existing business, your commitment and enthusiasm to what you are selling is essential for your survival in the marketplace. Your ability to market your products and services will determine the success or failure of the business; however, for that to be possible, you must be able to sell effectively to generate revenues and profits. **Karen Katz**, CEO, President and Director, Neiman

Marcus Group, Inc., once said, *"Selling is a skill to master. You will ALWAYS be selling no matter what you do."*

A sales strategy is not the same as a marketing strategy. Your marketing strategy should enable you to get your name out to your market and encourage your customers to buy what you are offering and your sales strategy, properly implemented, should generate increased sales and enable you to effectively establish yourself in the marketplace.

For a sales strategy to be relevant, it is important to have different strategies for each of your product lines, being conscious of the different customer groups or segments you will be selling to. Again, with the purchasing decisions of consumers changing constantly it is important to be continually evaluating your sales strategy to make it fit for purpose, enabling you and your staff to close as many deals as possible at every opportunity.

> YOUR SALES STRATEGY, PROPERLY IMPLEMENTED, SHOULD GENERATE INCREASED SALES AND ENABLE YOU TO EFFECTIVELY ESTABLISH YOURSELF IN THE MARKETPLACE

A good sales strategy must have certain elements to make it effective including:

- How to approach and engage a prospective customer professionally and with enthusiasm.
- How to showcase the value and benefits your product or service offers and how it can make your customer's lives better.
- The specific problems your product or service solves (good research on prospective customers should enable you clearly define these).

- The savings that can be derived from using your products or services, income to be generated or relief to prospective customers.
- Emphasize why you stand out against the competition and what makes you different from the others.
- How effectively your products or services help to better manage a prospective customer's life, process or business.
- Deliver a story that enables you to connect with the prospective customer as an individual rather than just being focussed on making a sale.

Incorporating these elements in your sales strategy will help you to build all-important trust with the prospective customer, enabling you to make a sale. However, a good sales strategy is only as good as the importance you and your employees attach to it and how clear or well understood it is by them.

> **A** GOOD SALES STRATEGY IS ONLY AS GOOD AS THE IMPORTANCE YOU AND YOUR EMPLOYEES ATTACH TO IT AND HOW CLEAR OR WELL UNDERSTOOD IT IS BY THEM.

SOCIAL MEDIA STRATEGY

The use of social media has become very prominent in marketing products and services in recent years and you do yourself a great disservice if you deny your business use of these great tools. It is important that a business considers social media as one of its most powerful tools in its marketing strategy because using social media effectively enables you to create a strong personal connection with your prospective customers and clients on a much larger scale.

Social media can be used to complement other methods of marketing and advertising without necessarily interfering with other media. The benefits can be tremendous but these tools must be used in the most efficient way possible.

It often goes like this, that as a business you simply sign up for any one of the social media platforms available, such as social networking websites, blogs, or video and photo sharing platforms, and build a following over time to gain awareness and to introduce the business to followers or subscribers. Although this sounds simple and straightforward, it can be very demanding if you are to make great success of it as a business.

Although there are niche platforms available, some of the commonly known platforms for business include, Facebook, LinkedIn, Twitter, Periscope, Tumblr, Pinterest, Google+, YouTube, Reddit, Slideshare, Whatsapp and Instagram.

The use of social media can provide a more personal touch in attracting potential customers. A good social media strategy will help your business by enabling you:

- To gain more traffic - Social media traffic is one of the biggest referrers of traffic to websites. Recent research showed that social media traffic made up 31% of overall web traffic. According to data collected by Shareaholic - a content amplification platform - from over 200,000 websites over the course of four months, Facebook alone accounted for up to 17.41% of overall traffic;
- To build relationships;
- To deliver better customer satisfaction;
- To retain customers;
- To deliver better customer care;
- To attract a more targeted segment of internet users;
- To get local and global exposure;
- To help you build a brand around your product or service.

Practically anyone can use the internet and can sign up on a social network website as it requires almost no special skills. Signing up to most of the websites and forums is free and it is therefore one of the cheapest ways of marketing. The return on investment, when used effectively, can be very high. This should be great news for any new or existing businesses with a tight budget. Of course, there is the need to keep up to date on how the various platforms are altering the algorithms driving their platforms in order to maximize the opportunity.

For a social media strategy to be effective there are a few basic points that need to be present.

- Understand and define who your target audience is and why they are on the platform or use social media at all.
- Explore, test and choose the most effective platform where your audience can be found and master the ins and outs of these platforms, taking into consideration that it will take some time to get it right.
- Create great content that delivers value to your audience and be consistent or regularly active or your chosen platforms. Content can be quotes, videos, blog posts, pictures, jokes, infographics, tips, discussion points, news events, and any other things that deliver value and enable you to engage with your audience.
- Actively go out of your way to get followers and engage with them while encouraging your followers to share your content as you build trust and relationships with them.
- Establish the best times and how many posts you can share on each platform to get maximum exposure and engagement. This is crucial because you don't want your subscribers to see you as a spammer because you post too many times a day or to ignore you because

you are not posting frequently enough. For instance, research by Buffer, a social media management platform suggests that on daily basis:

- ○ You can post 2 times on Facebook before likes and comments begin to drop off.
- ○ Engagement slightly decreases after the 3rd tweet on Twitter.
- ○ On Google+ you can post 3 posts per day, however, some users have noticed drops in traffic, up to 50% when posting less than normal.
- ○ You can post 5 pins per day on Pinterest, with an observation that, top brands on the platform have experienced rapid growth by posting multiple times per day.

To be effective you will have to research some of the existing tools like Buffer, Hootsuite, Shareaholic and others that enable you to manage your posts, drive more traffic to your website and, most importantly, track the results to understand what works best and tweak until you get the optimum result.

The whole strategy must be centered on sharing great content. Depending on the particular platform, you should be sharing a mix of old as well as new posts, promotional and non-promotional content as well as content from other sources to build up trust and followers and maximize your post exposure. It is the easiest way to attract more traffic.

A strategy that critically considers the above factors can yield a good ROI. Getting your network, subscribers and visitors to engage, and consistency in what works best for

GETTING YOUR NETWORK, SUBSCRIBERS AND VISITORS TO ENGAGE, AND CONSISTENCY IN WHAT WORKS BEST FOR YOUR BUSINESS, ARE KEYS TO THE SUCCESS OF ANY SOCIAL MEDIA STRATEGY.

your business, are keys to the success of any social media strategy. It will, however, require time, planning and execution to make it work for you.

Using social media has basically become the online version of word-of-mouth marketing. Using it in the right way will potentially result in more customers, increased sales, profit, growth and continuity of the business.

> USING SOCIAL MEDIA HAS BASICALLY BECOME THE ONLINE VERSION OF WORD-OF-MOUTH MARKETING.

For more on all the above strategies please check out my book "**The Business You Can Start**" where I delve into the various strategies into more detail. Available in both eBook and paperback formats on all major book seller platforms including Amazon, Kindle, BarnesandNobles, iBookstore and Smashwords.

CHAPTER 10

PASSION GIVES YOU THE IDEA, BUT DO YOU HAVE A SYSTEM IN PLACE TO OPERATE THE BUSINESS?

"Organize around business functions, not people. Build systems within each business function. Let systems run the business and people run the systems. People come and go but the systems remain constant"– **Michael Gerber**

For any business to find its footing and become an established thriving organization it must have strong operating systems in place. A successful business system should not be confused with a business model. A successful business system is simply how various aspects of the business interact and are operated and coordinated day-to-day to achieve the ultimate goal of the business. No matter how passionate an entrepreneur is about the business, without adequate systems in place the business has more chance of derailing than staying on course.

> A SUCCESSFUL BUSINESS SYSTEM IS SIMPLY HOW VARIOUS ASPECTS OF THE BUSINESS INTERACT AND ARE OPERATED AND COORDINATED DAY-TO-DAY TO ACHIEVE THE ULTIMATE GOAL OF THE BUSINESS.

A successful business system delivers significant benefits to the continued success of the business, including:

- Offering you a structured platform you can easily build on.
- Providing you with the freedom and ease to train others to operate the business even without your direct day-to-day involvement.
- Making it possible for you to confidently entrust your trained employees to manage the business while you focus on other important areas such as networking and building strategic partnerships for growth and expansion.
- Enabling you to easily identify what is working and what needs to be changed.
- Becoming the basis for your organizational policies.
- Helping you to expand your operations as you grow the business.
- Helping you to license your growing business to others as a franchise.
- Inspiring you to branch out into other lines of trade from what you originally set up to deliver.

What constitutes a successful system? Given the complexities of the types of businesses that exist I believe that every business should have the following core systems in place or at least have them in mind from the start to develop and build on. They include:

- Operations overview
- Administration
- Human resources
- Bookkeeping
- Marketing
- Sales
- Credit Management
- Debt management
- Customer care
- Supplier
- Payment

In creating a system, it is equally important to be clear on the processes involved in operating it. In the words of **W. Edwards Deming**, "*if you can't describe what you are doing as a process, you don't know what you're doing.*"

Although there may be other systems to ensure the smooth day-to-day operation of the business, I recommend those listed here as a starting point.

For a new business owner, managing all these systems may not be possible at first. Develop them gradually and allocate various tasks for different hours of the day or days of the workweek. For instance, some small business owners allocate the first hour or two of the day to email and correspondence, work on products or projects in the mid-afternoon, do filing in late afternoon, and catch up on industry news, social media updates and complete any reporting work towards the end of the day.

An existing business can also adopt this set of recommended systems to fully benefit from their advantages. For more details on the individual systems and what each comprise of please check out my co-authored book "**You've Been Fired! Now What?**" available in both eBook and paperback formats on all major book seller platforms including – Amazon, Kindle, BarnesandNobles, iBookstore and Smashwords.

CHAPTER 11

PASSION GIVES YOU THE IDEA, BUT DO YOU HAVE THE QUALITIES THAT SET SUCCESSFUL ENTREPRENEURS APART?

"Whenever an individual or a business decides that success has been attained, progress stops." – **Thomas J. Watson, Sr** - President of IBM, who developed IBM's renowned management style and corporate culture

Everyone goes into business with a desire to become successful, at least that is what I believe. However, irrespective of how passionate you are, the desire to succeed is not a guarantee of becoming successful. In this chapter, I want to discuss more qualities needed to be a successful business person so that you know all the factors, in addition to passion, that need to come together to give you the best chance of becoming successful.

There are certain characteristics and attitudes that distinguish those who have succeeded from those who are simply surviving or who have given up completely.

THE DESIRE TO SUCCEED IS NOT A GUARANTEE OF BECOMING SUCCESSFUL. IT IS THE STEPS AND ACTION YOU TAKE THAT GUARANTEES SUCCESS.

I must also emphasize that not possessing any one of these qualities does not in any way disqualify you from starting out or becoming successful as an existing business owner. I believe most of these qualities can be developed over time if you set your mind to it. Choices, not circumstances, determine your success. Here are some of the qualities for your consideration.

Desire. To succeed, you must have an above-average desire to break out of the 9 - 5 grind, to step off the employee-job-salary treadmill and to put your ideas, ideals and beliefs into action. Even as an existing business owner, you must be driven by a desire to work more than the norm on your business, especially in the early stages. **Eric Hoffer** stated, *"It sometimes seems that intense desire creates not only its own opportunities, but its own talents."* An entrepreneur's

> CHOICES, NOT CIRCUMSTANCES, DETERMINE YOUR SUCCESS.

desire for personal fulfilment and professional success is his or her number one key strength and the one that will force him or her to start out in business in the first place and grow it into a successful entity. In the words of **Napoleon Hill**, *"When your desires are strong enough, you will appear to possess superhuman powers to achieve."* Success can only be yours if you desire enough to act to achieve it.

Purpose. Successful business people have definite purpose in their lives. They know what they want and pursue it until they get it. In the words of **Vince Lombardi,** *"Success demands singleness of purpose."* The former British Prime Minister **Benjamin Disraeli,** also said, *"The secret to success is constancy to purpose."*

Decision making skills. Peter Drucker said, *"Making good decisions is a crucial skill at every level."* However, successful business people take this to another level by being able to make quick decisions when it's required and sticking by those decisions. Most of these decisions are not only based on facts but also on what they believe in or what their instincts tell them. You may not always get it right, however, following your instinct is a trait you must work on as it will be called on each day of your life.

Creative imagination. Successful business people are always creatively imagining scenarios and events. They peek into the future for ideas and solutions and this often makes them look a bit odd to the ordinary person as they seem to always float in their 'own world'.

Leadership abilities. To be successful is equal to being able to lead yourself and others to fulfilling a desired dream or goal. A good leader is firstly an active listener. A leader leads by example, whether intentionally or not. **John Maxwell**, a leadership expert, speaker and author, said, "*A leader is one who knows the way, goes the way, and shows the way.*" Also, in the words of **John Quincy Adams**, "*If your actions inspire others to dream more, learn more, do more and become more, you are a leader.*"

Self-starters. To be successful in business you need the ability to take the initiative and work independently to develop your ideas. Often, even the closest of friends and family may not see what you see. Do not wait on their approval or support before you set off because it may never come. People often jump on board only when they see you start. It is essential to be willing to walk alone until others catch up with you.

> SUCCESS CAN ONLY BE YOURS IF YOU DESIRE ENOUGH TO ACT TO ACHIEVE IT."

Higher goals. Successful business people are mountain climbers who, having climbed one peak, look beyond to the next highest one. They don't sit on their laurels or become satisfied with one achievement, they are constantly setting newer and higher goals. They are resourceful and proactive and rather than adopting a passive "wait and see" approach, they constantly work tirelessly to achieve their goals.

Self-determination. Successful people have strong determination to make things happen. A successful business person believes that the outcome of events is down to his or her actions rather than external factors or other people's actions. They don't attribute the failure of a task or event to others or shift blame.

Judgment. To succeed in business, you need to be open-minded when listening to other people's advice while bearing in mind your objectives for the business. You should have the ability to listen to other people's ideas without feeling intimidated or threatened. This is an attribute required to lead a successful organization with the ability to respect, tap into and utilize the unique talents of others in the organization.

Self-confidence. As a successful business person, you will need to have self-belief and confidence about your product or service. Your enthusiasm has the ability to rub off on your team and customers enabling you to win them over to your ideas, products and services. This also has the potential to inspire your team to have the confidence to deliver the best to customers, and for customers to develop the confidence to tell their friends and family about what you are offering.

Seek solutions in the face of problem. Successful business people are always looking at problems and challenges with a view to solving them instead of complaining about them or blaming others. **Paul Hawken**, entrepreneur and author once said, "*Good management is the art of making problems so interesting and their solutions so constructive that everyone wants to get to work and deal with them.*"

Commitment. Successful people are willing to make personal sacrifices through long hours of work and sacrifice of leisure time. They are unfailingly committed to whatever they are doing. "*There is a difference between interest and commitment. When you're interested in something, you do it only when it's convenient. When you're committed to something, you accept no excuses, only results.*" **Kenneth H.**

Blanchard. They can be counted on to get the job done and always make a positive contribution. "*There's no abiding success without commitment.*" **Tony Robbins**

Patience. A very interesting quality of successful business people, irrespective of their swiftness in judgment and decision making, is that they tend to know when to wait and when to act. Patience and commitment go hand in hand and the patient business people who dedicate themselves to working on their business day after day reap the rewards of their patience. As **Bill Gates** rightly puts it, "*Patience is a key element of success.*"

Realistic expectations. Ralph Marston once said, "*Don't lower your expectations to meet your performance. Raise your level of performance to meet your expectations.*" To be successful you will have to keep your expectations realistic. This is one of the best ways to avoid getting frustrated when things don't happen as quickly as you'd like them to which is one of the major causes of business failures in start-ups.

Risk. Another quality of successful business people is their relentless desire for risk. "*In a world that's changing really quickly, the only strategy that is guaranteed to fail is not taking risks.*" **Mark Zuckerberg**. Treading where no one has treaded before and taking up challenges others would run away from is what successful business people do best. However, they are more inclined to take a calculated risk than just any risk.

Perseverance. The ability to continue despite setbacks, financial insecurity and exposure to risk is necessary. Successful business people move towards the picture they create in their minds. They can rehearse coming actions or events as they "see" them and persevere until that picture becomes real. "*I do not think there is any other quality so essential to success of any kind as the quality of perseverance. It overcomes almost everything, even nature.*" **John D. Rockefeller**

Personal and professional integrity. Having a keen sense of integrity is important to ensure that business transactions are conducted ethically. **Don Galer** once said, "*Integrity is what we do, what we say, and what we say we do.*" A successful business person conducts him or herself in a respectable manner and always acts fairly and responsibly. **Richard Buckminster Fuller** stated, "*Integrity is the essence of everything successful.*" Those who ignore this principle regret it when everything they have built crumbles before their eyes when they are found out.

Driven by accomplishments, not money. Successful business people follow the theory of Apple Inc.'s founder, **Steve Jobs,** who said, "*The journey is the reward.*" They are customer-focused, not product-focused.

> SUCCEEDING IN BUSINESS IS MORE THAN BUYING AND SELLING PRODUCTS AND IT IS DEFINITELY MORE THAN HAVING A PASSION FOR BUSINESS OR HAVING AN IDEA.

Time management. Your ability to manage time is a key to being successful not only in business but in life. **Peter Drucker** said, "*Time is the scarcest resource and unless it is managed nothing else can be managed.*"

Succeeding in business is more than buying and selling products and it is definitely more than having a passion for business or having an idea. All the above qualities as well as those mentioned in earlier chapters influence a business person's ability to manage a business of any size at any level and still succeed, ensuring growth and profitability.

The truth is simply that if you are going to spend precious time and resources in stepping out and going into business, you must make every effort and resource count by using the right tools and having the right know how. Where you lack knowledge or skill in a particular aspect, make every effort to learn what you need to maximize the opportunity. Anything less is simply short changing yourself and wasting your time.

CHAPTER 12

PASSION GIVES YOU THE IDEA, BUT DO YOU HAVE A PLAN TO EXECUTE IT SUCCESSFULLY?

"If passion drives you, let reason hold the reins."
Benjamin Franklin

Any new business, start-up or existing business driven by a passionate entrepreneur aiming to become a sustainable success should have a realistic business plan regardless of whether it serves as a road map, is used to raise funds or to communicate the vision to customers, team and investors.

It has been said that, *"Failing to plan is planning to fail."* - **Alan Lakein**

The greatest benefit of the planning process lies in researching and thinking about your business in a systematic way. This is where I believe the real strength of the passion for whatever idea being pursued is truly stretched. Planning should help you to think things through thoroughly, study and research if you are not sure of the facts, and look at your ideas critically. **Dr. Graeme Edwards**, an international consultant, once said, *"It's not the plan that is important, it's the planning."* In other words, it's the "process" that offers the business owner the best shot at mapping out the best way forward before embarking on the journey.

A good plan can have many other benefits.

- It helps you to realistically weigh up the strength of your idea or opportunity.
- It serves as a guide or road map before even starting out, offering you and your team a clear sense of direction, telling you where you're going and how you're going to get there.
- It becomes a blueprint by which management and employees can fully understand and appreciate what the ultimate aim and vision of the founders are and how to contribute towards it.
- It helps you to prioritize and keep track of what needs to happen in order to achieve maximum success.
- It is a vital document when you're looking for funding – without a business plan you can't adequately assess your needs and convince potential lenders that your business proposal is achievable.
- It gives you something concrete against which you can measure your progress, keeping your company on track and in some cases it can help you avoid expanding too quickly which can have disastrous consequences for a small business.

A business plan also has both internal and external uses. For internal purposes:

- it can be used to help measure success;
- it can help you to focus on development efforts;
- it can help you to spot potential pitfalls before they manifest;
- and it can help you to structure the financial aspects of a business.

On the other hand, it is used externally to:

- introduce the business to, or apply for funding from, bankers, external investors (friends, angel investors, VCs), grant providers;
- introduce the business to potential buyers;
- and attract potential partners.

Ultimately the business plan is the best possible way to address all aspects of your business and must be comprehensive enough to help answer the following questions:

- What are the objectives for my business?
- How will I achieve these objectives?
- What are the risks involved?
- What is the timescale for major milestones?
- How much will it cost?
- Who are the key members of the management team?
- What products and services am I offering and what problems do they solve?
- What is the market size, who are the customers, competitors and what are the sales projections?

Clearly, the benefits of creating a plan to back your passionate idea far outweigh not having one because it is a document that helps you to articulate your ideas and research into a more structured format; clarify the purpose of the business; verify that the business idea is realistic and commercially viable; help set sales and financial targets; plan for the future of the business; and set out the business and marketing strategies. All of these factors are essential to help you to be equipped for the journey and not to be carried away by the excitement of pursuing what you love, only to end up with no business, because you did not consider the whole picture from the start. Planning is also key in ensuring the continuous existence of a business and every business owner should regularly review their business plan to ensure it continues to meet their needs.

Whichever way you look at it, the business plan is simply one of the most essential pieces of documentation that any person starting a business needs to put together. I sincerely believe that if you are truly passionate about your business idea, you will want to do everything you can to become successful and this should motivate you to plan before stepping out.

> THE BUSINESS PLAN IS SIMPLY ONE OF THE MOST ESSENTIAL PIECES OF DOCUMENTATION THAT ANY PERSON STARTING A BUSINESS NEEDS TO PUT TOGETHER.

CHAPTER 13

PASSION GIVES YOU THE IDEA, BUT DO YOU HAVE A GOOD FINANCIAL PLAN AND MANAGEMENT SYSTEM IN PLACE?

"Great businesses are built on great decisions, but owners really need to know where they stand today to make the right ones." **Bivek Sharma** - Head of KPMG Small Business Accounting.

Selling of products or services for profit is at the core of every successful business. However, to thrive in business, or even get to the stage of selling what you produce, requires more knowledge and understanding of how you manage the finances of the business.

The need to be financially prudent in managing your cash flow as well as other financial aspects of the business is crucial to your success. The only way to do that is by familiarizing yourself with the basics, such as pricing, margins, break-even point, cost of sales, gross profit/loss, overheads/expenses, net profit/loss, tax, borrowing, investing and, most importantly, your ability to keep a close eye on your cash flow. All of this starts with a good book-keeping system.

A good financial management system involves having a good understanding of cash flow planning and credit management and maintaining good relationships with your accountant and bank, after getting to grips on some of the components mentioned above.

Financial planning on the other hand, is the task of determining how a business will afford to achieve its strategic goals and objectives. Usually, a company creates a financial plan immediately after the vision and objectives have been set and it is often included in the business plan. Unfortunately, it is not uncommon to find most small businesses have no business plan, let alone a financial plan.

A good financial plan takes the actions described in the strategic business plan and, as addressed in earlier chapters, converts them into a monetary value. The financial plan will often describe each of the activities, resources, equipment and materials that are needed to achieve the business objectives as well as the timeframes involved.

> **A** GOOD FINANCIAL PLAN TAKES THE ACTIONS DESCRIBED IN THE STRATEGIC BUSINESS PLAN AND CONVERTS THEM INTO A MONETARY VALUE.

The accuracy of the financial plan depends on the quality of information used in the assumptions for the financial models. Creating realistic assumptions for key variables such as projected unit sales and pricing is critical for the ultimate success of the business and its ability to survive over the long haul.

At this point the question to answer is why financial knowledge and planning is something an entrepreneur or business owner needs to add to their passion and all that has been discussed above, to guarantee their business success.

Some of the reasons for good financial planning include the following.

- **Decision making** - It provides the numerical logic for the business owner in making better and faster decisions.
- **Confirms objectives** - It helps the business confirm that the objectives set are achievable from a financial point of view.

- **Set targets** - It is a means by which targets are set for employees to inspire and motivate them as well as the organization as a whole.
- **Focus efforts** - It shows where the business should concentrate its resources for maximum effectiveness in building revenues and managing costs.
- **Early warning system** - Checking financials regularly provides an early warning system for what is working and what is failing to enable you to put things right before it is too late.
- **Growth potential** - Efficient financial management enables you to identify where savings can be made, enabling the business owner to allocate more funds for marketing, expanding operations and product development, which in turn brings about more growth.
- **Long term view** - It allows the business owner to better see what expenditures need to be made to keep the company on a growth track and to stay ahead of competitors for the long haul.
- **Cash Management** - It provides the business owner with the peace of mind when the right structures are put in place to ensure adequate funds are available when needed. This enables the business to take advantage of opportunities that arise, such as the chance to purchase inventory from a supplier at temporarily reduced prices.
- **Spotting Trends** - It helps the business to set quantifiable targets that can be compared to actual results during the year. Trends in the sales of individual products can significantly help the business owner to make strategic decisions about allocating marketing dollars to maximize returns.
- **Prioritizing Expenditures** - The financial planning process helps a business owner identify the

most important expenditures, those that bring about immediate improvements in productivity, efficiency, or market penetration, versus those that can be postponed until cash is more plentiful.

- **Measuring Progress** - Particularly in the early stages of the business, where business owners are more inclined to work long hours, it can be difficult to tell whether progress is being made or whether the business is stagnated or eating into its capital with little or no profitable returns. Seeing that actual results are better than forecast can provide the owner with much needed encouragement. For instance, a chart showing steady growth in revenues month by month, or a rising cash balance, is a great motivating factor. The financial plan helps the owner see, with the clarity of hard data, that the business is on its way to being a success with a great potential to survive in the long run.

An entrepreneur or business owner's failure to manage their finances is the single most important factor that can sink the business. The consequences can be significant and more far reaching than almost every other point discussed above. Passion without a grasp on this all important factor is a limitation, and can undermine everything in the long run, if not kill the dream completely.

AN ENTREPRENEUR OR BUSINESS OWNER'S FAILURE TO MANAGE THEIR FINANCES IS THE SINGLE MOST IMPORTANT FACTOR THAT CAN SINK THE BUSINESS.

CHAPTER 14

CONCLUSION

"A business cannot survive on faith and passion alone, especially if you refuse to get out of your own way." **Alfred Edmond, Jr** - Black Enterprise Mentor

Up to this point it has been a forgone conclusion that passion is necessary in driving the entrepreneur or business owner on the journey to success. Just as **Dame Anita Roddick**, DBE, British businesswoman and founder of The Body Shop, once said, *"To succeed you have to believe in something with such a passion that it becomes a reality."* This further affirms the strength of the force of passion in the success equation.

> **P**ASSION IS NECESSARY IN DRIVING THE ENTREPRENEUR OR BUSINESS OWNER ON THE JOURNEY TO SUCCESS.

John Maxwell, an American author, speaker and pastor also once said, *"A great leader's courage to fulfill his vision comes from passion, not position."* Passion generates energy and excitement for

> **P**ASSION GENERATES ENERGY AND EXCITEMENT FOR THE TASK AHEAD.

the task ahead. Setting out to go into business on your own is a great decision but can be challenging, especially in the initial stages. Unless you are passionate about what you have on offer, you may not get anyone to want to even pay for it, let alone survive to succeed in it.

Again, it is equally important to note that if you are passionate about what you are doing then work should not be a struggle. Of course, there may be challenges along the way but the work itself can be a real joy because the passion you have for it, be it a business idea, a problem you desire to solve or a solution you are excited to deliver to potential clients, energizes you and drives you to go beyond your natural limitations.

> UNLESS YOU ARE PASSIONATE ABOUT WHAT YOU HAVE ON OFFER, YOU MAY NOT GET ANYONE TO WANT TO EVEN PAY FOR IT, LET ALONE SURVIVE TO SUCCEED IN IT.

However, right from chapter one, we have discussed why a business simply cannot survive by just 'following your passion'; passion is just one piece in the puzzle of what it takes to realistically succeed in business.

Although it can be said that most well-meaning business speakers, mentors and coaches, like myself, genuinely encourage audiences to follow their passion, this is just a starting point. Other qualities as discussed in previous chapters, including the presence of a genuine gap in the market, having the right mind-set, developing a plan, having good strategies in place, having great negotiation skills, cultivating the characteristics that enable business owners to become successful, creating systems, and having a grasp of financial management and planning, are equally important in building a successful business.

> IF YOU ARE PASSIONATE ABOUT WHAT YOU ARE DOING THEN WORK SHOULD NOT BE A STRUGGLE.

Without them a business owner or entrepreneur stands the chance of falling into the trap which has claimed many victims on this exciting trip.

Never in the history of the business world has there been so much knowledge, support and financial resources at our finger tips to set us up to succeed at anything we set our hearts to do. Yet many of us are not taking advantage of these factors, denying ourselves their immense potential to break new ground and give birth to new ideas and unique inventions, transforming the lives of generations unborn.

PASSION IS JUST ONE PIECE IN THE PUZZLE OF WHAT IT TAKES TO REALISTICALLY SUCCEED IN BUSINESS.

FAILURE IS AN INDICATION YOU HAVE TRIED, POTENTIALLY LEARNT FROM YOUR MISTAKES AND ARE READY TO TRY AGAIN.

The potential is there, the stage is set and even the resources to support ideas are in place. All it takes is for you to make the decision to step out and step up into what you believe is your destiny and make a go of it.

Yes, you may fail, so what? After all, failure is an indication you have tried, potentially learnt from your mistakes and are ready to try again. Don't forget that no one becomes successful at the first attempt. Just dig a little deeper and read about any successful person in any field and you will be inspired by the many stories of their failures and how they used them to propel them to change course, update themselves, seek out the right advice and prepare themselves to face their next attempt. And that, to me is the key.

NO ONE BECOMES SUCCESSFUL AT THE FIRST ATTEMPT.

If you have taken time to prepare yourself and work through what has been shared in the previous chapters, you will increase your chances of success significantly. That is largely because most of what has been shared is based on my experience from working with many entrepreneurs and business owners as a professional coach, mentor, consultant and business speaker, as well as my own personal experience as an entrepreneur over almost two decades. I have condensed all of this into the chapters in this book to provide you with a guide that I hope will inspire, equip and inform your actions on your exciting journey to success.

ABOUT THE AUTHOR

Victor Kwegyir is an international business coach and mentor, consultant, entrepreneur and the founder and CEO of Vike Invest Ltd, a growing International Business Consultancy firm in London, UK. He has over twenty years' experience in business, and holds a Master's in International Financial Systems.

Victor is a motivational speaker who has challenged and equipped people with the knowledge and practical tools in starting and growing successful businesses through his presentations at international conferences and seminars.

Victor is also a regular guest speaker and contributor to entrepreneurial development and business growth & profitability radio shows with over 70 guest appearances under his belt. He has his own blog and contributes to other blogs and business finance and management platforms, such as LinkedIn, StartUS Europe and other websites around the world.

In addition to this book, Victor is the author of:
- *"Pitch Your Business Like A Pro – Mastering The Art Of Winning Investor Support For Business Success"*
- *"The Business You Can Start – Spotting The Greatest Opportunities In The Economic Downturn"*
- *"You've Been Fired! Now What? - Seize The Opportunity, Creatively Turn It Into A Successful Reality"* (coauthor)

These titles are available on Amazon, Kindle, ITunes, iBookstore, Nooks, Sony Reader - eBook edition, Barnes and Nobles, Vikebusinessservices.com and book stores near you.

To request Victor for one-on-one business coaching, mentoring and consultation services, speaking engagements, ghost writing services and interviews please send an email to victor@vikebusinessservices.com.

Victor's books are available at special discounts when purchased in bulk for promotions as well as for educational or fund raising activities.

NOW THAT YOU HAVE STARTED YOUR JOURNEY TO BEING A BUSINESS OWNER AND ARE READY TO REACH FOR GREATER SUCCESS IN YOUR BUSINESS, DON'T HESITATE TO CONTACT ME IF YOU NEED HELP NURTURING YOUR PASSION.